INNOCENT KILLER

ROBERT L. ANDERSON

PublishAmerica
Baltimore

First printing

ISBN: 1-59286-712-X
PUBLISHED BY PUBLISHAMERICA, LLLP
www.publishamerica.com
Baltimore

Printed in the United States of America

DEDICATION

To all the soldiers of the Army Specialized Training Program
who were diverted from college and commissions into the
86th Blackhawk Infantry Division for combat in
World War II.

ACKNOWLEDGEMENTS

I would like to thank:

My wife Celia, who led me out of denial into talking about the war, prodded me into Mary Jane's class, read and edited my stories, and comforted me through the returning nightmares.

Mary Jane Roberts and the "Angels" of Emeritus College whose inspiration, encouragement and extraordinary wisdom helped me to unify my two worlds and to tell my story.

My son, Mark, and my daughter, Jill, who not only accepted my new truth but cheered me on.

My family and friends who read the chapters as they appeared and provided feedback, enthusiasm and helpful editing:

Jeff and Joan Anderson, Deborah Berger, Frank and Mary Blair, Michele Blair, Lili and Jon Bosse, Alan, Justin and Kate Cezar, Dianne Dias, Jerry Evans, Cassie Fitzgerald, Phil and Helene Green, Mary Herne, David Kinon, Carl Kugel, Skip Lindeman, Harlane Loeff, Ari and Bonnie Mark, Audrey Milholland, Ben Schley, Laurie Woodrow.

While the U.S. War Department's After Action reports and the 86th Blackhawk Division Association History helped refresh my memory in many respects they did not fill the gaps in recalling names of comrades. With that deficit and with respect for their privacy I have invented or changed names.

CONTENTS

OPENING DOORS

On the way home from my psychotherapy office in West Los Angeles, I didn't have to think about the route I would take; so one day, in this day-dreamy state, I found myself on a street that took me past a gun store. Made of solid concrete and with steel bars on opaque windows and a steel door, it begged for avoidance. This was not the first time I had detoured just to come by this building. I had actually done this many times through the years and always with the same feeling of curiosity, dread and excitement. I could visualize the rows and rows of rifle racks, pistol cases and shelves of ammunition. I always wondered if they sold M-1 rifles like the ones I carried in World War II, more than fifty years ago. As a psychotherapist for many years I could easily identify compulsive behaviors in others. At that moment I was shocked to realize that I had one of my very own. I was tired of letting my unconscious lead me around like this for so long and decided to change the pattern. I would either stop these mysterious side trips or park and walk into that stupid pile of concete and see what happened.

I had already driven very slowly past the building with impatient drivers honking their horns behind me, so I went around the block again and parked in front of the ominous door. I turned off the ignition, got out of my car and walked toward the door only to find my knees getting rubbery, and that it was hard to breathe. I was sweating and it was a cool day. I knew I was scared for some reason but I also felt I was doing something wrong. Was it my mixed feelings about gun ownership? I was against private ownership of any assault weapons and even preferred that private citizens not own weapons of any kind, except for me.

With the creaking metal door open I stepped inside and found the rows and rows of rifles and glass cases filled with pistols, just as I had pictured. A tall, beefy, sandy-haired man passing pistols back and forth with a customer said, "C'mon in. Look around. Be with you in a minute." The smell in the wood-paneled room reminded me first of my Uncle Warren's machine shop. Then came the seeping memory of the smell of weapons' rooms in various army camps with cosmolene storage grease and cordite, the after-smell of burned powder. Except for the blended-in scent of strong after-shave lotion, I felt curiously at home.

I ran a finger over the oily barrels of a row of antique rifles and shotguns while listening to the conversations of the three salesmen and their customers. All of the salesmen and two customers were former cops. Vince, the friendly man who had greeted me, was patiently talking to a very strange, disheveled young man in his twenties. This man glanced at me furtively and at the same time struggled to keep his mouth closed to hide his missing and discolored teeth. His skin was brownish-yellow and leathery. *Paranoid, schizophrenic street-person*, I thought, as he and Vince continued comparing relative advantages of Magnum, Walther, and Smith and Wesson pistols. *God*, I thought, *I hope Vince doesn't sell him a gun.* Then, suddenly, street-person asked to see a Luger and a P-38 from World War II and asked which was the best. Vince brought them out and I moved in for a closer look, feeling almost normal again. He said he felt there was no real difference. I heard myself saying, "Actually, Vince, the P-38 is far superior. It has a better compensated recoil for less kick, seldom jams with rapid fire and just shoots straighter."

Both men looked at me incredulously and Vince said, "Now that's amazing. That's pretty much what my father said once. How'd you know about that?"

"Well, I shot both of them quite a bit in World War II. Souvenirs, you know. Sold off my Lugers and kept one P-38." Then I moved off toward a display case of knives while the customer made his decision.

"I like the P-38, Vince. Will you put it away for me?"

"Sure thing, Carl. Anything else?"

"Nope, gotta go now. Good to see you Vince." With that, Carl was gone, pausing at the front door to peek into the street to his left and then to his right before stepping onto the sidewalk.

"Vince," I asked. "Are you really going to sell him that pistol?"

"No," he replied with a smile. "It's just a little game we play. He's an ex-con. I actually caught him in a burglary when I was on the force a few years ago and put him away for two years. Looked me up when he got out. I think I'm his only friend. Comes in every couple of days. Anyway, what can I do for you?" I was about to say I was just looking around but surprised myself by asking if he had any M-1 rifles. He said they usually kept four or five and led me to them. He lifted one out of the rack and handed it to me. I was shocked at how heavy it was. Eleven pounds with leather sling and bayonet, he reminded me. I had automatically held the rifle in the "port" position as he handed it to me. Right hand on the stock, just behind the trigger housing, and my left on the hand-guard in front of the cartridge chamber. Vince was delighted. "Damn!" he said. "You **were** in the war. My dad was too, and he taught me the whole manual of arms. Do you remember all that stuff?"

"Naw, it's been over 55 years."

"Hey," he said, playfully, "Try it!" Then with the same playful grin he commanded, "Order! Arms!" Both my arms moved automatically down and to my right, dropping the rifle butt alongside my right foot. Then my left hand moved back to my left side as I stood at attention. Without hesitation, Vince then ordered, "Inspection, —Arms!" My right arm lifted the rifle instantly at an angle across my body to meet my left hand again. But this time, after slapping the top guard, my left hand moved down along the rifle with my thumb engaging the bolt and jerking it into open position. My head dropped down slightly so I could check the open chamber to make sure it was empty, and then my left hand moved back to the upper guard.

Vince was delighted. "My God, I'll bet you haven't forgotten a thing. Now let's see you do the whole thing." Vince was warming to the challenge. I was back at Fort Benning, Georgia, following orders and watching my body respond, with no image in my mind about how to make these movements happen. "Parade rest! Atten-tion! Right shoulder-arms! Left shoulder-arms! Port-arms! Order-arms! Left-face!

Right-face! About face! At ease!" Between each of these orders, Vince fired quick questions and another security door deep inside of me started to open. Many of them I answered truthfully for the first time.

"Army?"

"Yes."

"Infantry?"

"Yes, 86th Blackhawks."

"Combat?"

"Yes."

"Kill anybody?"

"Yes."

"Anybody you shouldn't have?"

"Yes."

"Did you tell your family?"

"No."

"Close calls?"

"Yes."

"Wounded?"

"Yes, not seriously."

"Have a nickname in the army?"

"Yeah, Andy." I was winded, excited, disoriented and pissed-off. **I'm** the therapist, dammit. **I'm** the guy who badgers people all day to get them to face the truth and remember the past. Vince had just done a number on me and opened a door I had slammed shut a long time ago. I just wanted to get out of there until he said he had been in Vietnam, and that I was a lot like his dad. He said he had been very glad when his dad finally began to tell the truth about his experiences in World War II. He always felt his dad was holding a lot back when he just told the funny stories and minimized what it was actually like. He felt he would have done better in Vietnam if he had known what his dad had gone through.

"Why didn't you tell your kids?" he asked.

"Well," I said. "You probably know from your dad how in those days there was a kind of unwritten rule that we 'wouldn't bring it home.' It was really the 'manly' thing to do. Forget it, move on, get back into your real life. You complain in the army but not at home. I also didn't want my wife and kids to think of me as a killer. I thought they might be afraid of me and think what I had done was criminal. We all carried 'guilty' secrets that made us different from 'normal' people." Vince said he could relate, especially to the shitty things we had to do.

Then Vince had another inspiration. "Here," he chirped as he threw me another rifle. "Remember how to field strip this baby?"

"I don't think so, Vince, although I know I could completely dismantle and put it back together in the war, even blindfolded."

He said, "Let's see if your muscle memory holds up. I'll just start you off. Put the rifle butt on your left hip, trigger side of the rifle facing up. Now go!"

Without thinking, my left hand reached for the trigger guard, gave it a yank and pulled out the entire trigger housing. I watched in amazement as my hands then separated the stock from the barrel assembly. Next my hands grabbed the follower rod and spring assembly, pushed them back and slipped them out. After that I removed the bullet guide and operating rod catch. The gas cylinder plug was screwed out to allow removal of the front and rear barrel guards. Finally I rocked the sliding bolt and lifted it out. There was no way I could have verbally described what I did. Vince cheered and watched while I re-assembled the rifle.

While doing this, the benevolent blanket of forgetfulness began to lift. The gun an employee was test-firing in a basement room became the chattering of a machine gun. I pulled the trigger on the re-assembled rifle eight times, waiting for the ping of the ejecting empty clip. Images emerging in my consciousness were half-way between my body and my mind. There, hanging in a twilight fog, was the face of the first German I killed. There was Josh, blown to bits. My squad charging through rain and sleet. Buddies dropping and screaming. Was that a truck going by outside, or were artilllery and mortars dropping all around again? Then the door closed and Vince was looking closely at me saying, "You were back there for a minute weren't you? Happens to me all the time."

"Say, Andy," Vince added brightly. He had chosen to use my army nickname. "This M-1 was used in Europe — might have been yours, then sold to Denmark as part of a lend-lease program. Never used, but we bought it in perfect condition. If you want to buy it I'll take off two hundred dollars."

I said, "I gotta think about it." Then I grinned at him and said, "Vince, that's the one I want. Will you hold it for me?"

"Sure," he said and then, more seriously, he asked, "So are you gonna tell your family? I found, the more people I tell, the better. I don't even need drugs anymore." I said I was going to write it all in a book to my kids and everyone close to me. We shook hands and I told him he had been more helpful than he would ever know.

When I got home, I felt strangely relieved and in the weeks that followed I made contact with the 86th Blackhawk Division Association on the internet and received a copy of the history of the division. From the War Department I obtained a complete record of daily "After Action Reports" which detailed our forty-two days of combat in Europe. In my mother's belongings I found bundles of letters that I had written during that time. I looked through boxes of souvenirs which had been stored away for years, and rescued my uniform from a family of moths. I found the box of photos I had taken with my brownie reflex. I began talking to those close to me about what really happened. Some memories crept into consciousness quietly. Some leaped at me like avenging furies of hell. I began to write them down, one memory at a time.

While struggling for a sense of direction with the writing, my wife, Celia, placed a college catalogue on my desk, opened to the lead article about a gifted teacher named Mary Jane Roberts and her two classes on autobiographical writing. A week later I was sitting in class. As I began to share my stories with what proved to be a uniquely appreciative, encouraging, warm and intelligent group of peers, more doors opened. Mary Jane's wisdom, talent and ability to inspire, helped me to focus on the part of my life that most needed to be recovered and honored.

The two worlds I had so effectively separated are now joined in my story, Innocent Killer.

THE ANGELS OF LE HAVRE

I awakened slowly to complete confusion. I was in an iron frame cot. I looked up at a high-vaulted ceiling and then at the rows of cots, where olive-drab blankets covered sleeping forms. Pushing at the fog in my mind I found hazy, disconnected images of a large convoy under attack, seasickness turning to something worse, a navy medic blurting out, "Jesus,— 105 degrees," and being carried from my troop ship to a jeep. Then there was the ride through the bombed-out streets of Le Havre where grim-faced people threw garbage and rocks at us, cursing us as killers.

These images faded as I tried to turn from my left side onto my back and found I could not move. At the same time I became aware of a weight across my arms and my legs and something up against the full length of my back. I struggled against the constraints and heard a muffled feminine voice attempting to calm me. A woman was in my cot. A cascade of black hair fell on my face as she untangled herself from me and the blankets. She sat on the edge of the cot and looked down at me with a weary, warm and relieved expression. She seemed very young and beautiful. More angelic than medical. As she moved, a window high in the vaulted ceiling framed her head in a halo of light.

She placed her hand on my forehead as I looked away and met the vacant gaze of an older-looking GI on the cot about twelve feet away. As if reporting from a patrol, he quietly told me that I had been very sick, that I had been there for three days, that the young woman was our nurse and she had joined me in the cot to keep me from thrashing around and falling out of bed in my delirium. Then he said simply, "She's good people. Probably saved your life, she and penicillin. Doc says you had the worst strep throat he ever saw." The man shut his eyes, avoiding any response from me.

The nurse, obviously pleased at my return to consciousness was smiling and humming a French tune as she busily stripped off all of my clothes. She managed the turns of my weakened body with strength and gentleness. Then she was bathing me and helping me into a hospital gown of sorts. I found that her name was Danielle, that she was eighteen years old and not really a nurse. She lived alone with her mother in the basement of their collapsed home. Her father had been killed as a resistance fighter and her brother was serving in the Free French Army. She had volunteered at the little hospital when the Americans first arrived. She had a low soft voice and spoke a mixture of English and French that was easily understandable. On learning that I was nineteen she told me that I was the youngest patient and that she had been afraid that I wouldn't make it. Tears welled up in her tired brown eyes, revealing both her exhaustion and her caring.

Danielle told me I had been carried in unconscious on a stretcher on March 3rd and this was March 7th. She said she had been calling me "Robaire" since my name on the transfer order and dog-tags was Robert. I told her my nickname in my unit was 'Andy.' She decided she would call me 'Bobby.' I spent the next two days thanking her and watching in amazement and adoration as she took care of all fifteen of us. Her laughter dissolved gloom at each bed. I was considered contagious so my cot was located in a corner near the entry stairs, with my neighbor at least twelve feet away. His cot was the first of two rows extending to the end of the gloomy room. An improvised screen of hanging sheets separated me from the others.

As my head cleared and strength returned, I was able to shower, sit at a common table for meals and reach out for contact with the other men in the hospital. My farm-boy friendliness was met with annoyance and cool distance. They were all casually polite but they let me know that I was not in their league. All had been wounded and five had suffered limb amputations. Most were nearly recovered and ambulatory. There were two distinct groups, members of the 82nd and the 101st airborne divisions. By listening quietly and respectfully, I learned they had all been there since the Normandy invasion and surviving that, had all been injured in the Battle of the Bulge which was now in its final stages. Few made eye contact with me but one man did ask about my Blackhawk arm patch. When I told him it was a brand new division of eighteen and nineteen-year-olds called the 86th, there were no more questions. I longed for the camaraderie of my own outfit. My only real conversations were with Danielle who had become very precious to me. She took my letters to the nearby army post office and was sad that I got no mail. She was relieved to know that my letters from home were being saved at my company headquarters. After a week of isolation, Danielle removed the hanging sheets, in spite of Doc's orders and announced to the entire ward that I was well again

After my tenth day in the hospital the Doc, Lieutenant Jackson, gave me a pass to go out into the city of Le Havre for some exercise. Apparently I had also had pneumonia which more penicillin was curing. He only checked in about once a day. He never looked directly at anybody and was referred to as 'Dr. Jackoff.' I heard that he spent most of his time with a French girlfriend and selling supplies on the black market. He did manage to warn me about the townspeople's hostility toward GIs. We had bombed the city to shreds, killing an unusually large number of civilians. He gave me a map showing only two safe streets with a few friendly bars, cafes and sandwich shops.

On my first trip out of the hospital I was surprised to find no intact buildings, and that the street was filled with people pushing wheelbarrows full of bricks. People would walk to the other side of the street to avoid me. In a sidewalk cafe I found myself wondering if my ham and cheese sandwich might be poisoned. I had my first glass of beer and didn't like it. There was absolutely no one to talk to and I decided it was friendlier back in my depressed hospital ward.

In the hospital I found myself quietly studying different men. It helped me get past my feelings of invisibility and rejection. By listening and watching I felt I began to know who some of them were, even if they didn't want to know me. While pretending to be absorbed in a book Danielle had brought me, I strained to hear the men quietly talking about missed landing zones in Normandy. One of the men had landed in the center of a city and had watched most of his friends shot before they hit the ground. He had escaped by playing dead under his chute

17

until help arrived. Another man from the 101st spoke of being surrounded in Bastogne last Christmas when the Germans broke through in the Bulge. "We could have held out and beat the Krauts but that bastard Patton and his Third Army came roarin' in to rescue us — and we didn't need rescuing." I was in awe of these men. I had read of their stubborn fighting and refusal to surrender. They were referred to in the papers as "The Battered Bastards of Bastogne."

An 82nd man added his experience in a quiet, almost bored tone: "Well, we were to the north of you under Monty Montgomery's command, wanting to break through but that piss-ant wanted to just dig in and wait, as usual." They agreed that Patton was a bastard but they much preferred to follow him.

They all felt that Ike, for some reason, had given in to Monty over Patton and crippled our opportunity to make a major breakthrough. This somehow felt like information I shouldn't be hearing. Then I heard someone musing about something I thought I should hear. He said, "I was moving around taking shots at a small German patrol when I fired my eighth round and the clip ejected. While re-loading, they came at me shooting and got me on the side of my head. I was just laying there groggy and spouting blood when this arrogant Kraut who spoke English came up and told me how stupid GIs are. 'We listen for the "clink" when your clip ejects so we know when you're empty,' he bragged. Then they just walked off and left me there 'til one of our medics found me. Guess they thought I was dying." I realized, hearing this, that we had never been taught about that. I would have to pass it on.

Danielle was increasingly attentive and we enjoyed each other's company. Her affectionate gestures helped to ease the isolation of the hospital ward room. Once, when in desperation I had asked her why the men were so indifferent and unfriendly, she replied with amazing wisdom, "They have lost many friends so they don't want any more — to lose." Then matter -of-factly she said, "You will be leaving soon." She moved away quickly as if to spare us both the impact of our imminent good-bye. At this same time I had noticed a subtle mood change among the exhausted battle weary men. The pall of depression and disillusionment lifted a bit. I also noticed a very animated Danielle in the middle of several groups of men where the tone seemed unusually serious, all of them casting occasional glances in my direction.

I was stunned by what happened next. Early evening, after our meal, Danielle came to my cot, sat down and very calmly said that some of the men wanted to talk to me. My first thought was a fearful one. *What have I done? Did I offend someone? Are they angry that I am so friendly with her?* With an effort at bravery I said, "O.K." She motioned to the men and six of them came over to my cot, two of them thumping along on crutches and two, limping. Two men pulled a cot over to sit on and one sat on the foot of my bunk. The guys on crutches remained standing and slouched in a resting position. This was the first time that these men had actually looked at me. Danielle also sat on my cot and seemed excited.

In firm, measured tones the man nearest my cot who had given me my initial orientation began talking. He said, "You don't seem to know it but your life isn't worth a plugged-nickel unless you get out of here and back to your own unit right away."

The man on crutches with a missing leg added, "We know your story and we've seen it hundreds of times. You're separated from your unit and assigned to the hospital. You're just about well, and since your division is staging at Camp Old Gold outside Rouen and about to leave for the front, you're past history to them. You won't be sent back to the 86th. Instead, you'll be assigned to some other outfit at the front as a replacement."

"Where you will be assigned to the most dangerous duties," added the other man on crutches. "Unless you get to your division right away. Life expectancy of a replacement is about eight minutes in combat."

The man who sat on my cot reported calmly that he had scouted the rail yard while riding our supply truck and learned the location of my 86th division and the schedule of trains going to Rouen, which serviced Camp Old Gold.

My bunk neighbor with the vacant eyes took over and with a trace of enthusiasm said, "So here's the plan. Danielle is packing up your duffel bag right now and you will leave on our supply truck at 5:00 a.m. for the train yard. The truck driver will take you directly to an empty car on the train to Rouen. Get on and stay hidden 'til you get there. Then find an 86th Division supply truck going to your unit. They are all at Camp Old Gold and about ready to leave. You've got to go tomorrow." Danielle had placed her arm on my shoulder. No one seemed to mind. I stuttered my thanks in all directions and received some grunts and nods in response.

My 'older' bunk mate, who I learned was only 25 years-old, added with a grin, "You'll actually be AWOL but don't worry about it. Just get your company to sign you back on the active roster. They're so busy getting ready for combat nobody's watching little details like this." One voice back in the other group did call out "good luck." Otherwise there were no handshakes or goodbyes. I had my orders.

That night I was wide awake and all the men were asleep when Danielle came by and sat on my cot. Our longing for each other was overwhelming. I finally said I was afraid I would be falling out of bed a lot tonight. Without hesitation she was out of her clothes and snuggled up in the cot with me. Our passion seemed almost desperate as we clung to each other, as if this moment would never be possible again. We seemed as one, as we drifted between loving and sleeping.

The goodbye with Danielle in the morning was both painful and surreal. Our farewell hug and kiss was interrupted by the truck driver. She handed him a wad of American money from the men and my escape had begun. Unsmiling, bearded and with a seaman's cap pulled down to his piercing psychotic eyes, the driver sped through the city. Dodging bricks from newly collapsed buildings, but hitting every hole in the street, he took me on an early morning tour of a shell of a city. I wondered how anybody survived that kind of bombardment. At the rail yard he dropped me off in front of an open boxcar on a train headed east.

The weather was cold and the wind made it worse. I partly closed the sliding door and collapsed on a pile of hay, still very weak from my bout with strep. The first stop was Rouen where I jumped off with my duffel bag. 86th Division trucks were everywhere, loading supplies from the train. I flagged down one truck that was already loaded and after hearing my story the driver smiled and said, "That's the best story

I've heard lately. Hope they don't lock you up, Corporal." Then he told me to climb in. Later that afternoon I walked into the command tent of my company to the amazement of my officers and buddies. I described the details of my hospitalization and my unconventional departure, then asked for assignment back into my company.

Chester, our friendly company clerk, ended the puzzled head-scratching by addressing Captain Sullivan, "I'm right pleased to have Andy back Sir, I just added his name back on the roster. I doubt if'n anybody'll notice." Then, to me he added cheerfully, "Yer just in time for our train trip to the front tomorrow."

The Captain grinned and said, "Looks like you're in, Corporal. Better get some rest. You can get your rifle from the supply sergeant." I asked what day it was and learned that it was March 21st. I had been in the hospital fifteen days.

That night, in one of the tents of the vast tent city called Camp Old Gold, and with icy rain coming down in sheets, I told my squad my story. Jerry Sandler, my friend all the way from boot camp said, "You just beat being fresh meat as a replacement by one day, Andy. Man, you must have a guardian angel."

"Yep," I said, "fifteen of them."

CAMP OLD GOLD

By rejoining my 86th infantry division, I was back with my buddies, but I was also just in time to board a World War I troop train the next morning for the front. Camp Old Gold, with its thousands of tents appeared to be sinking in a sea of mud in a barren field fourteen miles out of Rouen. During those days in the hospital, my division had unpacked all of our equipment and had been issued the new leather combat boots and winter clothing. Although we had been trained for fighting in the South Pacific, the Battle of the Bulge had caused enough alarm in the War Department to re-route the Blackhawks to Europe instead. Friends in my radio squad had cleaned the cosmolene off of my rifle and drew clothing for me in case I returned in time. Wool pants and shirts, long-johns, wool knit caps to wear under our helmets and wool sweaters were a welcome exchange for our light-weight South Pacific clothes.

During my absence, my regiment took long marches in the rain through neighboring towns and practiced field problems when the rain stopped. Classes were held every day on the latest German combat strategies. There were also lectures on non-fraternization rules. Those boiled down to "No talk, no touch." Jerry, my quipping friend from Brooklyn, put on a resigned look and said, "Well, I guess all we can do is fuck 'em." He then proceeded to get me up to speed on extra-curricular happenings. For entertainment, there had been only a lone Red Cross truck with five women serving coffee and doughnuts in the evenings. They were not very friendly and hung out only with officers. A U.S.O. group had come through but decided it was too rainy and moved on. "Probably looking for the Air Corps." he added. "We missed you, Andy, but compared to us you had a vacation."

I liked Jerry a lot. His irreverent sarcasm and stinging wit had helped him survive the streets of Brooklyn where his parents owned a deli. He had helped me with his sardonic perspective on the absurdities of military life. He was only five-foot-five inches tall with large black eyes and thick wavy hair. His crooked mocking smile was tempered by the warm glint in his eyes. His cynicism was a good balance to my excessive optimism. I dreaded the day someone would beat him up, and he longed for the day I would "wake up."

Chester, our company clerk, stopped by our six-man tent with a large stack of letters from home, and as I thanked him, he sat down beside me on my mummy bag on the floor. He had been with the division long before our contingent arrived from Fort Benning. His scrawny body, long neck and round head seemed to fall naturally into a slouching "S" shape like the proverbial army "Sad Sack." G.I. clothes only made matters worse. He always looked as if he was wearing somebody else's. Collars were too large, sleeves too short. His pants and shirts, not knowing what to do with his oddly shaped body, just collapsed. His face was very round and filled with the largest and most infectious smile I had ever seen. Accompanied as this was by his ingratiating, warm-hearted friendliness, he was able to deflect most of the taunts and ridicule he had encountered in life.

Chester had grown up with poverty and brutality in an old-fashioned orphanage in the hills of Tennessee. Once, when asked if he smiled all the time, he had answered, "Yes, 'specially since I was drafted. I love the Army, and this here company, is my family." I found many things about him to be contradictory. From the neglect and harshness of his childhood he should have been angry and distrustful. Instead he was trusting, friendly and generous. He had a twangy, sing-songy, ungrammatical way of talking that suggested little or no education. However, in his job as company clerk he kept records meticulously, had an extraordinary memory for names and details and wrote memos and letters for the company commander in perfect English with correct spelling and punctuation. Also, while his incessant friendliness could be annoying, he was the only person who could calm our volatile First Sergeant Bruno. I had once asked him about the difference between how he talked and how he wrote and he had said, "I just remember everything a body ever tol' me,— 'specially in school. The way we spoke and the way we wrote,— them was jus' two different thangs."

Chester started to get up from the floor saying, "I best go so you can read them thar' letters." But then he paused thoughtfully at the tent flap as others in the tent chorused a, "Goodnight Chester," as they were drifting off to sleep or writing letters. But then, surprisingly, he came back over and sat down again. Leaning toward me, he lowered his voice and whispered with unusual seriousness, "Andy, ah hope you don't mind too much but I was listenin' when you was readin, parts of your letters to your buddy, J.C. and those t'others back on the ship. Ya know, where we was all jammed inta those seven deck bunks with no breathin room? Wal, ah ain't never hear'd people write or talk like that to each other. Like, they miss you and—and say nice things to you, —and tell you what they're doin,— and stuff like that."

"Chester, do you have any family at all?"

"Nope, none at all I reckon," he answered matter-of-factly. Even in the pale light of the candle I could see small scars of various wounds over much of his weathered face that I had not noticed before.

I said, "I don't mind a bit that you listened. In fact, any time I get mail just come on over and I'll read them out loud, or you can read them yourself."

He smiled awkwardly, stared at the dirt floor for a minute, then asked, "Andy, whada ya do with your letters when you're done with 'em."

"I save some and throw some away," I replied.

Pausing, as if waiting for courage, and with crimson flowing into his face he blurted out, "Would it be O.K. with you if I take care of the ones you don't want no more? I'd like to carry 'um around in my pocket like everyone else does and then I'd have letters to read after mail call."

It was only then that the sad paradox hit me. The man who made mail-call such a personal and playful experience for all of us by telling us who had written, sometimes by sniffing the fragrance of envelopes, and by knowing the names of all our correspondents, never received any mail for himself. I pulled out my pile of letters and asked, "Which ones would you like to keep for me Chester, the ones from my girl-friend or from my mom."

He answered quickly, "Well, if'n it's all the same to you I'd 'preciate your mom's. You see, I never really had a mom, so to speak."

I gave him four letters to "keep" for me. He thanked me with his well-known graciousness as I said, "Just let me know when you want some more to keep for me."

His smile returned to his face as he thanked me again and then, looking embarrassed, asked tentatively, "Oh, Andy, about the other guys...?"

"Don't worry, Chester, this is just between us." He nodded in appreciation and almost as an afterthought gave me two copies of phrase pamphlets, one for French translation and one for German, then disappeared through the tent flap.

As the tent quieted down, I opened my new mail and spent a couple of hours savoring each letter and writing responses, all by the light of one candle. I could see my mom and dad sitting at the kitchen table, sipping coffee, listening to the radio, sharing their worries and watching the tule fog form a nightly blanket over the vineyards. I could see my brother Herb, upset that his kid-brother was headed for the front while he safely trained marines on Guam. I wondered if the censors would let me get away with announcing our next movement by saying they wouldn't be hearing from me for a while. And then, thinking of Chester, I tried to imagine what it would be like to not have a family.

A conversational hum could be heard throughout the night as twenty thousand men attempted to relieve the mounting tension by swapping stories. Sleet pounded on our canvas roofs and the temperature drifted below freezing. The mournful playing of "taps" faded into the soggy night. Filling up on hot coffee helped keep us warm, but it also kept us up for many trips out of our mummy bags to our own private urinal. Leaving the relative warmth of our tent was avoided by somebody's brilliant idea: Attached to the center pole of the tent was a gasoline funnel stuck in the end of a long hose. The hose ran along the packed dirt floor and ended in a hole dug outside the tent. None of us were using the canvas army cots set up by the engineers. It was warmer sleeping on the ground wearing all the clothes we had, including overcoats and with spare duffel bags pulled up over the bottom half of our sleeping bags. Our duffel bags were packed and piled near the tent flap to be picked up in the morning and stored in a rear area. We had no idea when we would see our personal belongings again. The clothes we wore, combat pack and our weapons would be all we would have for the trip. Ammunition would not be handed out until we were at the front.

Josh, our high-speed radio operator from Oregon, burst through the flap of our tent along with a gust of cold air and shook the rain off of his rain coat. He had just finished a shift in the radio tent and said he had some news for us. During a lull in battalion radio traffic the operators swapped gossip. He heard that when the fighting stopped we would probably come back to Old Gold to pack up for home. There was no response as everyone was thinking the same thing — who would be missing when we saw Old Gold again.

When some of my squad members had fallen asleep, another close friend, J.C. from San Francisco, stopped in to welcome me back. We had been together all the way from our induction center in Monterey. He too got a lot of mail and was close to his family. Of all my buddies, he was the one I thought best qualified for O.C.S.. He was very intelligent and a natural leader. His hair was blonder than mine and we had about the same build, tall and slim. His eyes were blue like mine. He was also one of the few people in our company who passed the grueling physical requirements for the Expert Infantryman Badge. He was a combat telephone lineman in Corporal Brewster's squad. He lowered his voice and said, "Hey Andy, I don't know if I should tell you this or not, but you'll need to watch out for Brewster. He's still holding a big grudge about the fight you had back in Louisiana. Says you ruined his face and cost him his sergeant's stripes and that he's going to get you. Says he's going to get Colonel King too for taking your side in the court martial." Then he added reassuringly, "We'll all keep an eye on him. He's a real loose cannon."

BREWSTER

In the reveille formation everyone was present and accounted for except Sergeant Brewster, who was in the infirmary. First Sergeant Bruno announced with his sarcastic grin that a Summary Court Martial would take place in Battalion headquarters immediately after breakfast. I was to appear before our Battalion Commander, Colonel King, in a Summary Court Martial at 8:00 a.m. for physically assaulting a sergeant. I couldn't believe this was happening to me. I don't get into that kind of trouble. I knew the penalty would be time in the guard-house and loss of rank. It said so very clearly in our rules and regulations. As I thought of the humiliation for my family I began to feel ill. As Bruno droned on with the orders of the day for combat field problems, everyone's eyes kept drifting to the missing door of my six-man hut. Sergeant Brewster had taken the door with him on his way out, at the conclusion of our fight two days ago.

In the latrine and shower room, after formation, there were friendly greetings from the other privates. Most of the corporals and sergeants avoided being near me and their faces reflected both hostility and embarrassment. Word had spread that 'Andy' had knocked Sergeant Brewster through the door of his hut on Sunday afternoon. In the chow line for breakfast the Mess Sergeant splashed extra food in my tray and said, "You may need this today. I'm glad you whupped the cocky little bastard." I found little comfort in this since our Sergeant Steele hated everybody. I felt conspicuous in my dress uniform since everyone else was wearing fatigues. My squad surrounded me at our table and to my relief began trading stories about how to get 'laid' in Alexandria. The laughter loosened the unusually quiet and tense atmosphere in the mess hall. Supply Sergeant Bob Hartley stopped by our table on his way to the non-com table with a requisition for me to sign for a new helmet liner. Across the top he had written, "Good Luck." On my way to Battalion headquarters after breakfast, I stopped by the infirmary to have the bandage on my hand changed. A piece of Brewster's tooth had gone to the bone in one of my left knuckles and been removed.

I arrived early and found the answer to why I hadn't noticed Brewster in the infirmary. He was sitting there, in the waiting room, with a large dressing over one eye. Swollen lips exposed a missing front tooth, his left arm hung in a sling and he had a large bluish lump on each cheek and a black eye. He focused his one good eye on my bandaged hand for a moment then looked away. Two other privates arrived in dress uniform, and I was relieved to know I wasn't the only one in trouble today. After nods of compassion to each other I slipped back into my own private misery. I heard Colonel King in the inner room speaking above two other voices. My right hand was trembling. I tucked it under my left so it wouldn't be so obvious. I wished so many of my friends weren't on furlough.

Suddenly, the door opened and a clerk called my name. I was surprised that my legs worked as I stood up and walked into the room. The air was full of cigarette smoke and tension. I walked up to the large table and snapped to attention in front of Colonel King, "Private First Class Anderson reporting as ordered, sir." He returned my salute and seemed to look right through me with steely blue eyes. Captain Sullivan, my company commander, and Lieutenant Houston, our communications officer, were seated on each side of Colonel King. They acknowledged me with a nod and faint smiles.

Colonel King seemed frustrated and impatient as he started in on me. "Did you see Sergeant Brewster in the other room?"

"Yes Sir," I replied with a feeble attempt at calmness.

"Did you do that to him?" he asked with an incredulous tone.

"I guess I did, Sir."

Opening a file as he shook his head, he continued, "You're one of those Specialized Training Program people brought in from Fort Benning, Georgia when the government killed the program. You were sent here as a private instead of to college as a second lieutenant?"

"Yes, Sir."

"You got screwed!!"

"Yes, Sir."

"I see you were in company E at first. What were you doing there?"

"I was acting squad leader in the first platoon and trained as a sniper, Sir."

"How come?"

"I qualified as an expert marksman, Sir, with both left and right side."

"Why were you transferred to headquarters company? It says here it was the result of a Summary Court Martial. Jesus Christ! What the hell happened? Another fight?"

"No Sir. I was a day late in getting back from a furlough, and since a lot of guys were late, it was decided to make an example of us. No excuses were accepted. Lateness was considered AWOL and punishment was a transfer to another company or to another division as a replacement."

"Why weren't they harder on you?"

"I believe it helped that I had a letter from the station master in my home town about his error in calculating when I needed to leave for camp, and also that I had sent a telegram to my company commander. In looking over my record they noticed my experience as a telephone lineman and my radio licenses, so they transferred me to HQ company, Sir."

"Damn! Sometimes we do something right," he exploded and slapped my file down on the table. "Now, about this damn fight. We've already heard from Sergeant Brewster. I couldn't understand a damn thing he said with what you did to his mouth. Now! What the hell happened on Sunday afternoon?"

"Well, Sir, I was sitting on my footlocker in the corner of my hut writing letters when Sergeant Brewster yanked open our door and came straight at me, calling me every name I knew and many I'd never heard before. I knew he didn't like me but I hadn't realized how much he hated me."

Listening intently, Colonel King said, "I've heard Sergeant Brewster's eloquent profanity before, Private Anderson, but just give me a few examples."

"Well, Sir, it started with 'You fucking son-of-a-bitch, you think you're such hot shit with your big IQ'— went through a lot of insults about my girl friend, who's picture is on my foot locker and ended with threats of how he was going to 'cut me down to size, rip off my balls and stuff them down my throat.'"

"Then what?" sighed the Colonel.

"Then he demanded that I stand up. I knew he had been drinking and wanted a fight. He was actually frothing at the mouth and screaming at me. Three of my bunkmates raced out the door after trying to calm him down. I tried to reason with him and told him I had no wish to fight him. He then called me 'Chicken shit' and a 'coward.'

Colonel King, with his eyes blazing asks, "Weren't you ready to kill him?"

"No, Sir," I answered. "I was scared and I just wanted to stop him. But then," I continued, "He reached down, grabbed me by my tie and tried to pull me up on my feet. As he did, he cocked his right fist back and I knew I had to act. He had me in a corner. I couldn't even run by him and get away. I stood up quickly and brought my left fist up from the floor into his mouth as he was still looking down, then I followed with a right cross and a left cross, both to the face. He went down and was out cold."

Colonel King, looking curiously satisfied, said, "The sergeant said you hit him while he was down. Is that true?"

"No Sir, the floor was all that hit him."

"Then what happened? He said you hit him when he was leaving."

"Well, that's kind of true," I answered. "You see, I tried to revive him on the floor, with water from my canteen, and when he came to, I helped him up. He took a swing at me so I hit him again and that's when he fell back through our door, which was closed, and landed in the company street outside."

Colonel King cleared his throat and his blue eyes were twinkling, as he said, "We want you to wait outside for a few minutes, Private, while we talk this over. But before you go I would like to know how you knew when to open up on Sgt. Brewster with that 1-2-3 punch."

"Well, Sir, I was thinking of my father when I was sitting there and he always said, 'If you're ever cornered into a fight, wait till they make the first move, then make sure you hit first—and keep hitting.'"

The Colonel said, "I'd like to meet your father," then dismissed me to the outer room. Sergeant Brewster was gone and I could hear loud talking with bursts of laughter from the inner room. The clerk shuffled papers noisily at his desk trying to drown out the sounds. When I re-entered the room all three officers looked satisfied. Colonel King opened this meeting with a pronouncement to the world at large. "I've just gotta say," he began, "I hate it that there are cocky, self-righteous trouble-making little pricks like Brewster in my army and I hate that you had to become his victim and I hate it that through no fault of yours we are forced to discipline you. Now, we think we have found a way to do that and at the same time help you to regain your respect for non-coms." Lieutenant Houston and my company commander were openly smiling now.

"We have decided that your discipline will be a transfer." I stopped breathing as I anticipated a transfer back into a rifle company. But then Colonel King continued to say, "Your transfer will be from the lineman squad into the radio squad."

Lieutenant Houston added, "I have already scheduled you for radio operators school starting tomorrow morning." Colonel King said he had a recommendation from Sergeant Hartley that I also become the weapons repair person with the title Armorer Articifer which, he added, carries a corporal's rating.

"I have already approved your promotion and I plan to pre-date it to before your fight. So, since we have reduced Sergeant Brewster to Corporal it appears you didn't strike a senior rank after all. Good luck in radio school," he concluded. "You're my kind of soldier. Take the rest of the day off. And, Oh, Brewster has been told if he bothers you in any way he will be immediately transferred to another division. We feel that you took care of the main part of his discipline already. You're dismissed CORPORAL!" I thanked them, exchanged salutes and returned to my empty hut where I began a letter home.

"Dear Folks, you'll never believe what happened today."

THE WATCH ON THE RHINE

Hundreds of trucks struggled into the deep mud of our camp streets at four in the morning, jarring us awake in our cold, humid tent. The ominous howl of the engines and the eerie flashing of headlights on our tent jarred us back to the realization that we were now on our way to the front lines. Still wearing several layers of clothes, we lined up in company formation against the trucks. Rain mixed with hail created a strange growl as it landed on hundreds of steel helmets. First Sergeant Bruno strutted in front of us. Shouting above the engines and the rain, he seemed less belligerent than usual. The closer we got to the front lines, the happier he was. "He can't wait for some officers to get killed so he can get his field commission," Jerry yelled in my ear. Bruno said we would be lining up at the mess tent for breakfast, company by company, in fifteen minute intervals. From there, we would immediately load on the trucks for a short ride to the rail station at Foucart. We would board trains for an unknown destination, which we knew meant Germany. We had ridden many trains in the States, and imagined that warm coaches and cushioned seats would be waiting for us.

As we pulled alongside our train, there was complete silence in every truck as we all stared in disbelief. "They gotta be kidding," gasped Marco Santini.

"My God. They're the size of my train set at home," J.C. added.

"Looks like thar's a car fer each of us," Chester chirped optimistically.

"Forty and Eights," someone announced, "From the first World War. The French hauled forty men and eight horses in those things." I told everyone that my Uncle Ernest had ridden on these with horses when he was with the U.S. Cavalry. The tiny, flimsy, wooden boxcars were strung together for as far as we could see in the early morning light. A coal-burning steam engine hooted off in the mist. Sliding doors were open as we all climbed in, about thirty-six men to a car. Inside we found two bales of straw, a large case of "K" rations and a container of water. It was going to be a long ride.

On March 22, 1945, our unlikely relic of a train creaked and groaned into motion as we spread out the straw and settled into a variety of uncomfortable positions. Never able to exceed twenty miles per hour, our two day, 350 mile trip seemed like an eternity as we headed east and a little north through northern France, Belgium, Holland and into Germany. Towns made famous in two world wars were on our path: Camri, Mons, Namur, Liege, Masstrict and Aachen. Rain seeped in through the splintered siding and roof and then down our helmets. I sat near a large hole allowing me a good view of the countryside. As we passed through Holland I saw a group of crashed gliders mostly under water in large tulip fields. I had read of many such casualties of the D-Day invasion.

It was almost impossible to sleep with someone else's boots in my face. And even though we had periodic stretch stops we cheered the announcement that our Regiment would de-train in Aachen and board trucks for the thirty-eight mile trip to Cologne on the Rhine River. Our elation was quickly dampened by the fact that we were now in the combat zone. This was also where the Germans had been stopped in the Battle of the Bulge. Our airborne and other divisions had pushed the Germans through Cologne and across the Rhine. No rear-echelon units had moved in yet to occupy Aachen. It was completely deserted.

Shaking the straw out of our clothes, we marched into the city for the exercise and to meet our trucks. The searing odor of rotting bodies hidden under debris hung over a completely destroyed city. We were wide-eyed and silent as we walked in double columns through the rubble. In spite of the graphic training films I had seen in training, I wasn't prepared for this. As I stepped over and around bricks, I could see clothing, kitchen utensils, family photos and children's toys. Dead cats and dogs were everywhere. In the street there were shell holes from mortars and large artillery. Shrapnel fragments were stuck in shattered trees and burned out buildings. We passed barbed wire barricades, burned out Sherman and Tiger tanks as well as disabled vehicles of all kinds. Contents of bombed buildings, including apartments and homes, were scattered everywhere. This was the aftermath, and we were headed into the actual conflict itself. I had felt fear before in my life but never anything like this. Shivering, heart-pounding, cold sweating terror held me like a vise. I clenched my teeth and brought on a toothache. I moved automatically, thankful that someone up ahead was shouting orders as if he knew what he was doing.

The trucks were waiting for us on the outskirts of the city. They were a welcome sight even if they were headed for Cologne. Progress was slow as the drivers dodged destroyed vehicles and shell craters. Signs of more recent fighting were everywhere now. Churned up earth was fresher, dead horses and cows were decaying in the fields, dead German soldiers and some civilians, including children were lying by the side of the road. Our first view of death in the war. At one point we were routed by MPs onto a narrow, alternative road just outside Aachen.

After a few miles, Marko, standing at the front of the truck and facing forward shouted, "Jesus Christ, guys, Look! It's the god-damned Siegfried Line. We're going right through it." We all jumped up and stared out at the bombed-out pillboxes on either side of a roadway that had been scraped out by tankdozers. Jerry told us that the reinforced concrete was about six feet thick. Only direct hits by bombs and our heavy artillery could knock them out. Our trucks slowed as they passed through the four rows of pyramid shaped tank obstacles which we learned were referred to as dragon's teeth. These had been built in front of the pillboxes. We also learned that these fortifications were connected by underground tunnels and trains. "Must have been one hell of a fight," I found myself saying to no one in particular. As we approached Cologne on the evening of March 27th, we could see large bursts of light across the entire horizon, followed by muffled explosions which grew louder as we neared the Rhine. We passed our own artillery groups returning the German artillery fire. We were at the front.

Now reduced to a snail's pace, we found the reason was that some elements of the 8th Division, including some walking wounded, were already evacuating the city. They were walking slowly as if in a trance, in two columns on each side of the road. They were battered and exhausted. An awkward quiet fell over each truck in our convoy as we moved through them on the road. The contrast was unnerving. In my clean, warm clothes, with letters from home in my pocket, with my stomach full of food and riding in a covered truck, I found it hard to look them in the eye. They had been to hell and we had not. The men passing by us also stared straight ahead in worlds of their own. They looked like men from a different army.

Somehow, in the lead truck, we felt the need to relieve the quiet disparity as quickly as possible. I was no help, locked in speechlessness, but Jerry came to the rescue by shouting to those nearest us on the road, "Hey, Mack, did you leave any for us?" The response was immediate from the straggling columns on each side of our truck.

A few voices found the energy to shout back, "You'll be sorrrr--yyy," a phrase we were all accustomed to hearing at any 'changing of the guard.' Then, suddenly and more seriously, a rapid exchange of information took place.

"How long you been on the line?"

"Forever!"

"Are the Jerries giving up?"

"Not so's you'd notice."

"How bad was it?"

"Reeeal bad. Their 88's killed us. They shoot on a time-table. Learn it."

"Many casualties?"

"Yeah, 'bout half."

"Any pointers?"

"Yeah, go home."

"How's the night life?"

"There're some women'll trade for chocolate if you don't mind gettin' the clap."

"O.K. Thanks, Mack."

"See ya, Joe."

About then, I noticed one of the men on our side of the road, limping, his head bandaged and his arm in a sling. He looked familiar and I called out, "Richards! Hey, Rich Richards, it's Andy." He looked up and his grimace turned into a smile of recognition. My friend all through boot camp and Company 'E,' he had grown up in a small town near my own. When I was transferred to Headquarters company, he had been part of a group taken from the 86th and sent to Europe as a replacement. Like an idiot, I asked, "How are you?"

"Never better," he replied. "How do you like my new outfit?" He cut off my apology and anticipating my question said, "Some Kraut got me with a grenade. The son-of-a-bitch gave me a ticket home." We were shouting now as our columns moved in opposite directions.

"See you when we get home," we both yelled.

Cologne was gutted in much the same way as Aachen and Le Havre, but this time there was a reception committee, the men of the 8th Infantry Division. We took over an area just two blocks from the Cologne Cathedral. The Germans across the river knew something was going on and also gave us a reception with increased shelling. The timing and shelling patterns were recorded and passed on to us so we would know when it was safe to move about on the streets. The veterans of the 8th seemed fairly blasé about the explosions, even the ones that were close. It was hard to believe that someone was really trying to kill us.

That evening before we officially relieved the 8th, our cooks set up in a concrete public building and served a hot dinner. Mess Sergeant Steele who always smiled when he was swearing at us announced to everyone in line, "Now if any of you High-Q babies complains about what I've cooked, you're goin' to be findin' some very interesting things in your food from now on." Sgt. Steele would never let us forget that as Army Specialized Training transfers, we were not welcome. He also called us "egg heads," and proclaimed that we had no "common sense." The safest response was to just look at him blankly and move on while he would answer for us in his perpetual psychotic dialogue. "Oh, please, Sgt. Steele, now you've hurt my candy-ass feelings."

After dinner most of my company assembled behind the mess building where our chaplain was holding an inter-faith service.

Everyone came and formed into rows, sitting on helmets. Captain Sanders, our chaplain, did parts of the service in English, Latin and Hebrew. I didn't hear much of what he said but I found his calm, steady reasonableness very comforting. As he mentioned the war, shooting, inevitable dying and duty, much of the terror seemed to fade. Just hearing those words spoken with such calmness and matter-of-factness seemed to remove the panic I was feeling.

Colonel King, our battalion commander, spoke to us at the end of the service. He said, "Men, I have never felt as confident going into battle as I do with you. This is an outfit with guts and brains. Yes, we will have casualties but I want you to know that this Regiment is invincible. When we take over tomorrow, we're going to terrorize the enemy. We're tough and we'll only get tougher. We're going to hit and run, in just one direction. We are here to end this damn war. Tomorrow morning the 8th pulls out and we take over. We'll be here a few days ducking their artillery and chewing them up with ours. We'll do patrols at night to find the best place to cross the river. Then we'll go get 'em. See you in the morning." That night we had our first two casualties. Two men on late night guard duty, circling the block in opposite directions bungled the password exchange, panicked, and shot each other.

It was March 29th when the 8th Division pulled out and left us on our own, facing the German Army with the Rhine river between us. Amazingly, we suffered no casualties from the carefully-timed shellings. We did have casualties from some of our night patrols who went across the River in rubber rafts to assess activity on the eastern bank. I welcomed the opportunity to get used to the sounds of combat before being in the thick of it. I soon knew the different sounds of artillery and mortar shells and could tell the difference between the German 20 millimeter and 40 millimeter fire. More than anything, I hated the screaming whine of the 88s. When I knew the difference between 'outgoing' and 'incoming' shells, I didn't have to dive for cover as often.

I felt lucky not to have been picked for river-crossing patrols at night. Those were handled by our Intelligence and Reconnaissance guys who were especially trained to locate, capture, and interrogate enemy soldiers, especially officers. Regular shifts of guard duty in bunkers along the river, alternated with shifts on the radio, became almost routine. With my free time I explored the city along with my buddies, J.C., Jerry or Marko. There were almost no civilians in our sector and not one intact building. I doubted that such a devastated city could ever be re-built. One day, Jerry and I decided to visit the Cathedral. Machine gun fire from across the river was aimed up the streets on each side of the Cathedral. About five short bursts each hour. Always on the hour. After the fire we just walked across the large square in front of the church and took each other's picture in front of a burned out German tank in front of the entrance. Inside the Cathedral we could see that our bombers had scored direct hits. In spite of this, the ancient building seemed indestructible. We went a little ways up the stairway in the south tower but quickly found a mountain of debris and turned back. Before descending, I looked out of a glass-less window and saw the collapsed Hindenberg bridge leading to the east bank of the Rhine. In the gray mist I could see scattered flashes of German artillery and mortars as they lobbed shells into the city. Back on the street we crossed the square before the next German barrage. I wondered if the Germans would always be this predictable.

My toothache had caused some swelling in my jaw and even though it was getting better, I decided to see if they had a dentist in the first-aid building. I was soon in a field dental chair, with a second lieutenant poking around my sore gum. He never actually looked at me and completely ignored my yelling. His breath was so foul I stopped breathing for as long as I could. Then he muttered, "May be an impacted wisdom tooth. Looks like you've been grinding your teeth. Not bad enough to dig it out now. Come back if it gets worse. Sure you're not just trying to get out of combat?" Then he just walked out saying, "I need a drink."

In my letter to Mom and Dad that night I mentioned that we had gone through the Ardennes where Uncle Ernest had fought in World War I. I was sorry that I hadn't found out more about what really happened to him. I just knew he had been in the trenches, saw many men die and was gassed. Not quite ready for sleep, I looked at all my buddies scattered around the basement of our bombed-out building and realized how lucky I was to be going into battle with them, instead of as a replacement in another division.

Only a week had passed since I had said goodbye to Danielle who had probably saved my life, not once, but twice. First, by her care in the Le Havre hospital and then by stirring up the paratroopers to help me get back to the 86th Blackhawks. I felt ashamed that I hadn't thanked her enough for all she did. Then I remembered a 101st trooper thanking her in the hospital one day and hearing her scold him, "Sergeant Jim, you have it the wrong way. It is I who say thanks. You drove out the German pigs. You gave our freedom back. I can never repay enough." I went to sleep knowing I wasn't the only one in love with her and decided I would find out how to write to her and send her something from Germany. Chester would know how to do this. As everyone quieted down we could hear the low-powered buzz of a German reconnaissance plane that we called "Bed-check Betsy," making it's nightly circle over Cologne to check on the status of the west bank. We had long ago given up taking pot-shots at the sound and became believers in the fact that a rifle bullet cannot bring down a plane even though Sergeant York did it in World War I.

While drifting off to sleep my thoughts went to Uncle Ernest and the stories he told me of life in the cavalry. No gory details. Mostly about how cold it was through two winters, how hungry they would get and how the Germans used gas on them. Gas masks didn't help much and he had been very sick. He always chuckled when mentioning that the wind changed and blew the gas back at the Germans. I wondered if they would ever use gas on us. I wondered if I would come out of this war 'shell-shocked,' the way he was, and be mad at everybody.

Cologne Germany, 1945

Cologne Cathedral

Services before the first day of combat, outside Cologne

UNCLE ERNEST

Uncle Ernest, who lived with us on the ranch, was not only Dad's partner and a cranky veteran of World War I, but he was our nanny. I had the dubious honor of being the favorite of all his nieces and nephews. That was because he was a constant source of entertainment and I followed him around all the time waiting for something to happen. Especially when he tried to fix things. He called me his shadow and thought I liked him. So his stinging criticisms and commands were milder with me. The truth is, I wasn't so fond of him. I just watched for the inevitable mishap, when I would learn some new swear words and see God punish him for his meanness.

In his part-time work at the Model-A Ford agency Uncle Ernest was a legend. He ran the parts room in the service department and took me to work with him sometimes. He knew the name of every part of a Ford. If they ran out of a part, he knew how to make something else work. I was impressed and proud. Sometimes he would upset my dislike for him by bringing me a present, like stacks of empty boxes-within-boxes from the parts department. A sure-fire way to distract him from lectures on my behavior was by asking for the story of his childhood. He relished telling how he was born in a cave and helped his Swedish immigrant parents build a sod house on a homestead in McCook, Nebraska. He had also helped build the house I grew up in near Kingsburg, California.

If I was especially good to him and stopped tormenting my older brother after dinner at night, he would bring out his war chest. Choking through the wave of moth-ball fumes, I would watch and listen in wide-eyed wonder as he laid out his uniform, steel helmet, leggings, mess-kit, army blanket, bayonet, medals and a heavy trench coat. The climax of this ceremony was when he reached under his bed and brought out the 30-06 Enfield rifle that he carried through two years of trench warfare in France. I heard of frost-bite, bad food, dysentery, charges on horseback in the Ardennes and transportation with his horses in railroad cars carrying forty men and eight horses. Sometimes, majestically, he would put on the uniform and go through the manual-of-arms enjoying my fascinated silence. The bond I formed with my Uncle contributed to a long-time loyalty to Ford cars, horses and the army, and to my ability to get along with very difficult people.

I was about eight years old when I realized that Uncle Ernest, who had been gassed in World War I, was seriously funny. Not to him though, just to those around him. The only time we heard him laugh was when he was listening to Amos 'n Andy on the radio. He could draw wide-eyed amazement and snickers from both children and adults, with his uninformed but authoritative proclamations. "Kids who don't study in school should be in reform schools or put to work in the fields," he pronounced in one family gathering. This was just one of a long list of his suggestions on child-rearing. I had asked, "Do you mean me, Uncle Ernest?"

"'Course not," he answered indignantly. "You've just got ants in your pants and you don't pay attention." I knew he didn't mean it because I was his favorite.

Uncle Ernest respected my father, adored my mother, and functioned as a kind of Sergeant-At-Arms for our nuclear family. My brother and I prayed for the day he would marry somebody and move out. We had figured out that our Dad, in his great wisdom, nearly always made the right decisions in everything. We thought it was because he would hear Ernest's opinion and then do just the opposite.

My parents' efforts to soften Ernest's constant judgments, criticisms and indignation helped very little. His very reputation provoked challenges. Teenage boys from town would speed by our ranch stirring up dust, waiting for their prey to shake his fist in the air in impotent rage shouting, "Gol-dang, carn-sarned kids!" With that reward, they would turn around and speed by twice as fast, giving him the finger and taunting him as the dust enveloped him. Uncle Ernest preferred animals to people. "You can train them, they respect you and they don't talk back," he proclaimed with satisfaction. One morning, when we were all in the barn milking cows, my older brother Herb and I began our game of squirting long streams of milk into the open mouths of about fifty barn-cats as they all sat up on their haunches, in a long line. Catching what they could of the moving stream, they then licked the spilled milk off of each other.

As expected Uncle Ernest roared his disapproval, "Stop wasting milk you gol-danged wastrels, and stop playing. You'll spoil those carn-sarned cats and they won't hunt." We buried our heads in our cows' flanks, above the udder, and squirted carefully into the buckets between our knees. Then he got up from his one legged stool, came over, and told us to tighten the hobbles on our cows or they would kick us over and spill the milk. We pretended to do so but left them as they were. He gave his cow an impatient shove as he sat back down on his stool. She lost her balance, the hobbles slipped off and she kicked his stool out from under him. He went down as his bucket of milk spilled all over him. Turning almost crimson, he got up fuming, grabbed the stool and whacked it over the cows haunches and jerked the hobble chains so tight the legs were almost together. "See what can happen?" he snapped as he began milking.

Suddenly his cow mooed in distress, hunched up, slipped out of the hobbles and kicked his stool out again in such a way that he slipped into the gutter behind her. As "carn-sarns" and "gol-dangs" flew, he scrambled to get up just as the cow looked back at him, raised her tail and dumped a huge load of green diarrhea all over him. Herb and I were convulsed in giggles and decided we had better punch each other in the arm in order to look serious as we went to help. We couldn't wait to grab a hose and wash him off with freezing water as he struggled to get up from the gutter. We apologized for the cow, "She's sick, Uncle." We always apologized for whatever he was upset with. It seemed to work the best in calming him down. We also knew never to refer to these incidents again, except with Mom and Dad.

Later that same day, after school, Herb and I were out in the vineyard checking the irrigation ditches to make sure water was flowing where it should. We took a running jump across the four-foot-wide ditch to check a leak on the other side. As soon as we landed we heard a yell from Uncle Ernest to "Hold up."

Herb muttered, "Now he's going to tell us how to irrigate."

In his raspy, agitated voice our uncle shouted, "Didn't anybody ever show you kids the right way to cross a ditch?" He stood his shovel on the ditch bank to catch his breath and it promptly fell into the water. Fishing it out with a snort he stuck the spade in the center of the ditch and grabbed the wet handle with both hands. Then in his tight, patronizing tone he instructed, "Now you stand on this side of the ditch, use the handle to support you, and swing yourself over to the other side, like this." With that he pushed off, and in mid-air his hands slipped and he splashed down full-length in the muddy water. We helped fish him out as he berated shovel-makers for making such slippery handles. We apologized for the shovel as he grumbled his way back to the house for more dry clothes. Herb and I crawled under a grapevine and convulsed as quietly as we could.

When we came in for dinner, we walked past Dad replacing a manifold cover on the tractor. He was tightening the last bolt as Uncle Ernest came up with a very large wrench and told Dad that he could never tighten those bolts tight enough with that small wrench. Dad, graciously stepped aside as Ernest applied his wrench and promptly twisted the head right off of the bolt as he skinned all the knuckles on his right hand. As expected, the wrench went flying, right through both side windows of the hay truck twenty feet away. Dad, with his infinite patience, told his brother to go take care of his hand and that dinner was ready.

Herb and I followed Dad to the kitchen and found Mom eagerly waiting for news of our day's adventures. Dove-tailing our sentences, we poured out the latest reports on our Uncle, while our folks responded with familiar amused expressions that accompanied the words of sympathy. Then, Mom, as expected, reminded us, "I know he can be difficult boys, but remember, he was gassed in the war."

Uncle Ernest Milking Time

BAPTISM OF FIRE

On April 4th, the 82nd Airborne Division sauntered into the center of Cologne to relieve us. As a squad of paratroopers came down the stairs into the basement of our bombed-out building, they looked like the ones needing relief. Their distinctive arm patches reminded me of the wounded guys who helped me so much in the Le Havre Hospital. From their conversation as they settled in we learned that the 101st Screaming Eagles were relieving other 86th units strung out between Cologne and Bonn along the Rhine River. I also knew that both paratroop units had been in the thick of it since the invasion, including the Bulge and Bastogne. One guy with a black beard and a dirty bloody bandage around his head growled, "First time up?" When we all nodded he said, "Pack all the socks you can steal. You'll sure as hell need 'em up in the Rhur where yer'goin."

The squad leader, called Joe by his buddies, pulled out a half empty bottle of whiskey, took a long swig and without choking added, "Don't be surprised that we know. We just got back from a recon jump up near the Rhur. Worst landing I ever had. That dammed Black Forest. Got caught in the trees. Climbed down part way and fell the last twenty feet. Fog and rain at the same time. Krauts everywhere. More infantry, artillery and tanks than we could count. We brought back one of their Generals so G-2 probably got all the info they needed. Count on it, that's where you'll be headed." His offer of a drink felt much like a cigarette being offered to a condemned man. Having had his fun scaring the hell out of us he proceeded to say, "But don't worry, you'll have a ton of divisions going up there with you."

Lieutenant Kramer, our platoon leader, dropped by at that moment to announce that tomorrow we would load up in jeeps and trucks and cross the Rhine on one of several pontoon bridges. Our engineers had

48

built them during the last two days under constant shelling. However, our patrols across the Rhine last night reported that the Germans were retreating, leaving only rear-guard snipers to slow us down. We learned that our 1st and 3rd Armies had already crossed the Rhine to the north and to the south of us, and had encircled the huge German force of nine divisions and three Panzer divisions in the Rhur. We were to drive a little north and east toward Siegen, following our leading Regiment to help mop up the city, and then attack all the way to Hagan to close the pocket from the west. And if possible, keep moving and cut the pocket in half. We would have air cover and the support of some tank Corps and Artillery units. We were now attached to the 18th Airborne Corps of the 1st Army. Lieutenant Kramer made communication assignments and I found I would be in the radio jeep with three other operators until we met resistance. Then we would be on foot with walkie-talkies, one of us with each platoon. We all knew that when we were not on duty with our specialty we were to function as infantry riflemen. We were to draw bandoleers of ammunition, grenades and 'K' rations tonight and be ready to board vehicles at 0600 hours tomorrow morning.

"Tomorrow we meet the Krauts face to face," he added. "Personally, I can't wait. I'm sick of sitting around dodging their artillery. Oh, and get your letters written early. Chester will come around later tonight to pick up mail. Get some sleep men, God knows when you'll get another chance."

Later, with our piles of ammunition and grenades resting on our combat packs, we focused on our weapons. Knowing we would be using them tomorrow, we were furiously field stripping and cleaning our M-1 rifles, 45 caliber pistols, M-3 machine guns and M-1 carbines. I tried to imagine how it would feel to see someone shooting right at me and my shooting at him. Although the phrase formed in my mind that "I might be killed," I wouldn't believe it, even though my stomach jumped every time I thought of it. The cold shivers up and down my spine bothered me even worse. Killing someone didn't seem quite as upsetting, partly because I hated Nazis and maybe because killing animals had been a necessary part of life on the ranch. I never liked it though, shooting bob-cats, rabbits and squirrels to protect our crops. I also hated killing horses and cows when they were injured or too sick to recover. We all fell silent, afraid to reveal fear in our voices.

In my letter to Mom and Dad, I knew I mustn't tell them how I really felt. So it went like this, "We're supposed to jump off tomorrow for a little more action but as you know, I'll be pretty safe as a radio operator, so don't worry about me. Germany is such a beautiful country. Too bad it's run by that monster Hitler and his Nazis. It's April Mom, and I'll bet your gardens are already blooming. I'll really miss the lilacs on my birthday. Had a letter from Herb. Glad he's safe on Guam training marines. Corporal Brewster still hates me but nothing to worry about. We just avoid each other. Margie writes great letters almost every day, just like you guys do. I love your letters. I really like it when you add something too, Dad. May not be able to write for awhile as we'll be on the road. Love, Bob."

With my letter finished I was re-reading some letters from my Mom, Margie, Herb and my favorite Uncle Vern, who taught me to shoot. Chester came bounding down our stairs with his usual smile and cheery greeting. "Well, I hear tell we're goin' on an outin' tomorrow and I want y'all to be kerful 'cause yer my family, ya hear?" He picked up our letters and paused as he studied the address on my letter.

Then quietly I said, "Oh, here, Chester," as I handed him a small packet of letters from my folks. "Will you keep these for me?"

"Ah shore will, and thanks," he replied and carefully slid them into his field jacket pocket as he waved goodbye.

It seemed that only the paratroopers were snoring that night. The rest of us were up and down all night for pee-breaks and to re-check our weapons. With maybe a couple hours of sleep we were up before daybreak organizing our combat packs. A last hot meal was served by our cooks, as the caravan of trucks rolled in to pick us up. Bombed-out buildings shook and walls collapsed as our convoy roared past. Fog had rolled in and a heavy icy rain was falling as we headed south along the Rhine toward Remagen. The canvas top was up on the jeep I had been elected to drive, but a cold wind blasted the rain through the sides and glistened on our dark green raincoats. The river seemed peaceful and very full and wide. Just when I was thinking that Chester was right, this was like an "outing," we passed through Bonn, another ghost of a city. We speculated among ourselves that we might be heading for the famous Remagen bridge that had been saved just as the Germans were all set to blow it up. However, just a few miles before Remagen we turned east toward the river and saw the pontoon bridge with engineers waving us onto the entrance. And then we looked up into the sky.

A swarm of German Messerschmitts circled like vultures in the mist waiting to swoop down on the bridge. This was it. We were in it now. Our convoy of jeeps and trucks was directed by engineers to cross the bobbing snake-like bridge one at a time between strafing runs by the planes. Two jeeps were already in the churning river after stalling and being pushed off the bridge. Divers were in the freezing water anchoring the jeeps for later rescue. I drove the jeep right up to the engineer with his arm in the air while my three squad members were welding their fingers to the hand rails. Then as a plane went swooping by with machine gun bullets punching holes in the water, the engineer dropped his arm and in a bullhorn voice yelled "Go!" With a stranglehold on the steering wheel and all four wheels fitted into the aluminum channels across the rafts, we were in a race for our lives. The strong current and the weight of the jeep created a strange bucking motion as I accelerated. Certain that at any minute we would be thrown off of the bridge, I floored the gas pedal as two planes bore down on us with machine guns spitting bullets and tracers that kicked up tails of water toward us. The bullets were zinging into and off of the metal channels behind us as I pulled onto solid ground between a couple of buildings and began breathing again. The throbbing ache in my jaw told me that I had brought on a swelling of my impacted wisdom teeth.

On the sloping east bank and under some trees lay a row of dead engineers, killed during construction of the bridge. Beyond that were the G.I. casualties from the assault unit that had forded the river in rafts to secure space for the building of the bridge. Dead German soldiers were scattered on each side of the road as I raced to catch up with the convoy. Behind us we could see that some of our planes had arrived and engaged the Messerschmitts in brief dog-fights before the German planes retreated. Our progress on the road was slowed considerably by the ever-swelling columns of refugees heading west for the Rhine. As we were often forced to stop, we spoke to some of the refugees who spoke English. We were told that most were escapees from Nazi work camps and included people of many nationalities. There were some Wehrmacht deserters, and German families whose homes had been destroyed. Some were in carts drawn by a variety of animals, but most were walking, carrying large bags and suitcases. Many avoided eye contact with us, even when we handed them our cigarettes and candy from 'C' rations. I couldn't even begin to understand all the reasons they had to distrust everyone. On one of our stops, Colonel King came by in his jeep to tell us that the Germans were building up for a fight in Siegen and that we would approach on foot through the fields outside of town. Another of our Regiments would lead our 86th Division along with the 97th Division in the first assault, and the rest of us would follow to clean up what was left or missed. His final words as he drove off were, "They know they can't win but they can't decide whether to keep fighting or give up. Let's help them make the right choice." I wondered if he remembered me from my court martial hearing, back in the States.

As we swept through several towns heading for Siegen, I became aware of the startling beauty of the country and the meticulous grooming of the roads and fields. Roads were often like green tunnels through dense forests interspersed with clear areas of rolling green hills. In village after village we found most buildings flying a white flag. All residents were off of the streets and watching us gloomily from windows. Children seemed less fearful and often appeared outside as we roared through their towns. We rewarded them with 'C' ration candy bars. We were often moving too fast for extensive house-to-house searches.

Nearing Siegen, we watched our planes overhead on bombing and strafing runs toward the city. We also passed long-range artillery, lobbing shells into the city ahead of our troops. As a result, the horizon was filled with brilliant flashes of color enhanced and carried out to us by smoke and misty clouds. The sound was a continuous roar which faded as we approached the field outside the city. We left our vehicles and forming a column on each side of the road advanced up a hill through very dense forest. Swirls of fog were like luminous ghosts in the light rain. We could hear shells going both ways overhead. Had this forest been cleared? Nobody knew.

As my infantry company approached the front line of combat for the first time, our terrified silence was shattered by the squishy thump of a German bullet tearing through the chest of Jack Kline directly in front of me and a second shot hitting the man behind me. The sound of the rifle followed. Our two columns dived for cover in the ditches beside the road, landing in freezing water. Captain Sullivan, our company commander, passed the word that a sniper had been missed by the company ahead of us. Three men were assigned to move ahead to locate the sniper while we waited. Our medic, Marty Stone, quickly checked the two men lying on the road. His message to us was clear as he stuck the rifle bayonets into the ground with their helmets on top.

The stark reality of combat descended on us as we heard another sniper shot and then a long burst from a Thompson sub-machine gun. Two of our men came back from the surrounding forest dragging the third who then became the third casualty on the road. The sniper had been left where he fell. The "move out" order was passed along and we returned reluctantly, to the road, in our quiet double column moving toward the heavy fighting going on just over the next hill. Artillery and mortar shells and the distinctive sound of hand grenades punctuated the constant chattering of machine guns. A road sign announced the city of Siegen. My friend J.C. commented from behind that my luck seemed to be holding. I felt a stab of guilt as I wondered why I hadn't been hit.

The explosions over the hill were reflecting off the dark, rolling storm clouds, as we moved up the hill and then slowly down to a field a mile outside the town. The battle was now in the town. I felt we had dropped into the very jaws of death. The road was lined with the still forms of dead G.I.'s, rifles with helmets askew serving as temporary headstones. The field, with a couple of hedgerows, was pock-marked with shell craters and strewn with the bodies and parts of bodies of both German and American troops. Dead cows and horses and even some sheep were scattered around the field, bloated and with legs stiffly outstretched. The smell we had noticed for a couple of days on the road could now be identified. It was the smell of death, now almost suffocating.

Adding to the macabre scene surrounding us, was the sight of our company mess truck set up at an intersection to serve us a hot meal at the outer edge of the field. As usual our cooks were snarling at us for keeping them waiting as they dropped mashed potatoes, roast chicken and canned peas into our mess kits. Until then, my only interest was in survival along with an overwhelming desire to run into the woods and dig a hole ten feet deep to crawl into. Somehow the presence of momentary hot food and our familiar cooks brought a bit of bizarre comfort, although no one could think of eating.

The rain began to pour down, flooding our mess kits just as the battle came to us. Artillery and mortar shells from a battery on the other side of town sent a barrage into our intersection. Mess kits went flying as we all tried to get away. I sprinted into the open field, dodging human and animal bodies as I ran. The explosions were all around as shrapnel whistled by and bounced off of my helmet. Flying clods of dirt felt like shrapnel. One knocked the wind out of me and I was sure I was badly wounded. Cries of "Medic! Medic!" were everywhere. I dived under a truck in the field in sheer terror but when someone yelled that I was under a gasoline truck, I got up and ran again, diving for a shallow crater as more shells began to fall. A shell went off so close I was completely deafened and lifted almost two feet off the ground. When I landed, I saw Robby Jenson lying next to me, blood pouring out of his shoulder and ear. He was moaning for his Mom. The shelling stopped briefly and I reached out and grabbed his hand. His arm came loose from his shattered shoulder. Others on the field were screaming in pain as Marty and another medic raced around injecting morphine in the injured. Marty threw me a tube of morphine which I injected into Robby, just as the other medic arrived and pronounced him dead. As we rallied to help the twelve wounded to the roadside for ambulance pick-up, it seemed as if we were all covered with blood, twelve from serious injury and the rest of us from minor shrapnel cuts and from the men we were helping.

As survivors, we were back on the road with orders to enter Siegen for a house-to-house search for German soldiers who survived the first wave attack. By now most of us were fed up with the interference of our bulky gas masks and tossed them in growing piles along the street. A blue-gray haze of gun powder and dust hung over the formerly picturesque village. We formed up by squads on the outskirts after looking over a rough map of the town. Each squad was assigned a street to clear. I led a squad up the street with my heart pounding so hard I was afraid everyone could hear it. I tried to slow my heartbeat by reminding myself of our training for such an assignment.

My first building was a garage with doors closed. We were divided, six on each side of the street. One man opened the door quickly at my signal, with others at rifle ready. A stocky German soldier was standing inside looking visibly surprised, with his rifle pointed at me. I shot first and his shot went into the ground as he crumbled slowly to the ground, a haunting look of shock and disbelief in his eyes. My other squad members fired at the falling man as if to release their own terror. I felt relief to still be alive but could not even begin to deal with the fact that I had just killed someone. Combat numbness had begun. We moved up the street, alternately leading and covering. At one house a German soldier opened the door and immediately put his hands up. In the adjoining garage we found a dead soldier wearing an iron cross around his neck. He had been dead for sometime and was covered with flies.

We could hear occasional M-1 shots on other streets and assumed other squads were finding soldiers hiding. Most doors were opened by terrified owners when we pounded on the doors with rifle butts. One German family heard us coming and eagerly opened the door before we knocked. They led us in where an older man sat holding a shotgun on a German SS officer. We took him outside as he smirked at us arrogantly. Then he made a quick move to grab Charlie's machine gun but Charlie twisted away quickly and emptied his magazine into the prisoner's stomach as they wrestled. One of the bullets passed through the officer's body and into Jerry's canteen which now squirted water down his pants leg. The rest of us had been slow to react and I vowed never to let that happen again. Charlie was unconcerned about any of this but did say, "Sorry Jerry," and simply leaned over, yanked the Iron Cross from the man's neck, and plunked it into his pocket as we moved on through the town.

Three soldiers surrendered to us in different homes without resistance. We just opened doors and there they stood with their hands on their heads. All together our Regiment captured about 200 prisoners, which were sent to the rear under guard. We re-formed our company on the other side of town as the sun was going down. Orders came to move right on into the field, this time as the leading edge of the attack. One Regiment veered off to our left and another to our right. Three regiments, of about twelve thousand men, spread out in a wide assault formation for as far as we could see. There was no longer any question. This was clearly the front line and the Germans were waiting for us somewhere in that field and in the city beyond. Attendorn was our next major objective, with several towns in between.

We soon approached a deadly hedgerow. It was almost dark. The only sound was the sloshing sound of our combat boots full of rain water. The Germans behind the hedgerow opened up on us with machine guns. Men fell and dove for tall grass. The screams for "Medic!" began again. We crept close enough to see forms to shoot at. I saw the helmet fly off of the one I aimed at. Lieutenant Kramer yelled for the walkie-talkie I was carrying. I knew I had to run over to his shell hole but with the machine gun bullets popping all around overhead, I paused, waiting for the Germans to cool their guns. Then, I counted to three, jumped up, ran five paces and dived into Kramer's crater as the popping started. As I ran, I heard a voice saying, "Dear God, please don't let me die." It was my own voice. Kramer called for sixty and eighty millimeter mortars behind us to plaster the hedgerow. The mortar shells with their high looping trajectory were soon dropping behind the barrier. When they stopped, we moved close enough to lob hand grenades over the top. Then there was quiet. The word came to dig in for the night. This was my first foxhole on German soil, a slit trench about six feet long and eight inches deep, that would get me below the surface of the ground.

Rolled up in my wool overcoat and rain coat, I covered myself with my shelter-half and some brush and took a first shift on guard duty. I felt a twinge of hunger but didn't have the energy to open the wax-covered 'K' ration in my pack. I had used almost eight clips of ammunition. Plenty left for tomorrow, I hoped. I had passed my first test of combat. I didn't freeze, I didn't run away and I had been able to kill. But what about tomorrow? Would I be killed? Even though I was warmer now, I was still shivering. *Can't think about it. Think of something better.* Someone was singing, "Someone's in the kitchen with Dinah—" I tried to join in but no sound would come out. I thought of Mom and Dad sitting at the kitchen table listening to the radio. I realized it was April fifth there too, and our orchards were beginning to blossom. It had been a year and a half since I had left home for Fort Benning, Georgia. Mom wrote me almost every day and Margie, who was becoming my girlfriend, wrote very often. Her letters were filled with passionate promise and made army life bearable. How would they feel when their letters were returned? Dad would take it the hardest. I remembered finding him once sobbing on our back steps when he found out that he would have to borrow money from the bank again to provide for us and keep the ranch running another year. I couldn't imagine how he could deal with word of my death. *There's just one thing to do*, I decided. I had to stay alive. An hour and a half later Chester's voice called out, "Andy, get some sleep, I'll take the next watch." In spite of artillery barrages to our left and right, I slipped into a stuporous kind of dreamless sleep.

Next morning we peeked over the row and I saw the second person I knew I had killed that day— a young, teenage German boy in uniform. My numbness deepened as we formed up to walk to the next town, wondering how to deal with having become a killer.

LEAVING HOME

The early morning chill awaked me to the realization that by tonight I would be in the Army at the Presidio in Monterey, about three hundred miles away. Before this I had only been to San Francisco, San Jose and Santa Cruz, all less than four hundred miles from our ranch, near Kingsburg. And that was to visit family. I felt the same mixture of excitement and fear that I always had before playing in a football game or team-roping with my brother in rodeos. I was also relieved. The waiting was over.

It was October 19th, 1943, and most of the guys my age and older were already in some branch of the service. Most had skipped their senior year in high school and enlisted in the Marines and Navy. Frank had already been wounded twice in the South Pacific. I wrote him about how I regretted passing the Army Specialized Training Program test given to all senior boys, which committed me to wait until I was drafted. It felt even more shirking and unpatriotic to be sent to *specialized* basic training and to college, instead of into combat. His response surprised me. "Don't be stupid. Do anything you can to stay out of combat. There's no glory here. Stay in school. You belong in the Signal Corps or Army Band. Just don't date my girlfriend." I still felt guilty. Going on to school, even through the Army, still felt like a chicken-shit way of staying out of the real war.

The familiar orange glow of sunrise poured into my upstairs, corner bedroom as I looked out over acres of green vineyards sloping gently to the tree-lined Kings River at the foot of our ranch. Between the vine rows were wooden trays. I had helped the Hernandez family field-workers fill them with Thompson seedless grapes now drying into raisins. The peach crop had been picked, cut and dried by mid-summer. The harvest was finished and our pickers had struck their tents and returned to Chandler, Arizona for the winter. They would store their colorful tents until next summer and move back into a real house. I wondered if they would still dance, sing and play their guitars the way they did every evening around a campfire in our orchard. Dad had announced at dinner recently, after paying Jesus Hernandez in cash, that we might actually do a little better than break even this year.

As I lay in bed between the cool, smooth sheets, I found myself unusually aware of everything. I heard myself saying, over and over again, "I'm leaving home, I'm leaving home," and wondering why the thought didn't bother me more. Outside my window mockingbirds were competing with new melodies. Our cows, waiting for the gate to be opened into the pasture, were complaining. Blue Jays screeched as they dived for tufts of hair from our unsuspecting cats. Our two-story white and gray farm house creaked and snapped, as the sun warmed the wood siding. A tractor whined and chugged in a distant field. I always liked knowing that I was born in this house that my grandfather had built forty years ago. I guessed it would be here when I came back. If I came back.

Best of all were the familiar sounds of my father and mother talking in the kitchen below as they prepared breakfast together. Their conversation, while usually buoyant and fun, was different this morning. It was subdued and without the spontaneous bursts of laughter and song that were so much a part of our life. They were preparing in their own way for today's short drive to Parlier, where I would take a Greyhound bus to Porterville to join other draftees for the ride to Monterey.

Knowing that I wouldn't see this room again for a long time I found myself looking at each thing as if for the first time, not so much to say goodbye but more to absorb it and take it with me. Knotty pine wallpaper covered the walls of a room too small for my hobbies. There was my short-wave radio station, drum set, saddle and bridle, swing record collection, stolen stop-sign, cardboard figure of the Lucky Strike cigarette girl, hunting rifles, pole climbing spikes and belt for my part-time telephone lineman job, and a work-bench for my radio repair business stacked with radio chassies that I used for spare parts. Little room was left for a small dresser and mirror. A full-sized Brahma bull-hide fitted snugly on the floor as my carpet. Pictures covered the walls. On my cowhide-covered chair Mom had placed my freshly ironed sport jacket, shirt and slacks.

I had sole possession of the upstairs with three bedrooms and bath. Herb had been away at college for two years in the Marines Specialized Training Program. His vacant room, still kept ready for his visits was next to mine, neat and uncluttered in stark contrast to the chaos in my room. The juke box we had bought for ten dollars stood in the hallway between our rooms filled with the latest from Glen Miller, Benny Goodman, Gene Krupa and the Dorseys. From the sudden pause in the conversation downstairs I knew that someone was coming to awaken me.

There were several ways Mom and Dad had of calling us to breakfast. The usual was to open the stairway door for my dog Rusty, who would run up the stairs, jump onto my bed, and pull the covers off with a triumphant growl. Then he would repeat his ritual with Herb if he happened to be home. Herb was not as appreciative of Rusty's early morning enthusiasm as I was. Another was to trigger the juke box to play one of the current top tunes. The more personal wake-up calls would include Mom playing a Souza march on the piano or Dad yelling one of his Swedish expressions up the stairwell meaning, "It's a beautiful day if everything goes well."

This morning it was Mom calling my name sweetly and somewhat tentatively. "Bobby, breakfast is ready." When I came into the kitchen, Dad was already seated and Mom was at the stove.

"So, Son, are you ready for today," Dad asked, as he pulled out a chair for me.

"I really am, Dad. It's been pretty hard this summer, running into people in town and everyone asking when I'm going to be leaving. I was glad when the city band concerts were over in August. I was about the only young guy left in the band."

"Did anybody ever say anything?" Dad asked, ready to rise to my defense.

"No, but you know how people are in town, they smile and are friendly but you never know what they are really thinking. Anyway that's all over. By tonight I'll be in uniform."

"Oh, by the way," Dad added, "Uncle Ernest said he's proud that you're going into the Army. He said to tell you to make sure you get shoes that fit. You'll be doing a lot of walking."

With everything on the table, Mom joined us and wanted to know what would be happening at the Presidio. I told them I thought it would be like a preview of boot camp, where they teach us to march and salute and stuff. I also knew we would be taking all kinds of tests to find out who we are and what we can do. I was excited about getting my summer and winter uniforms, but had heard we wouldn't get our weapons until were assigned to our boot camp. I wasn't looking forward to the work details, like k.p., cleaning latrines, making beds and picking up cigarette butts. I understood that when I showed them my letter about passing the A.S.T.P. test, I would be routed off into a special O.C.S. type of basic training. Mom sighed a big sigh and said, "I'm so happy that you took that test. I always hoped you could go to college. I would hate it if you were going right into combat."

As we sat around the kitchen table looking out over the vineyards, Dad said our usual blessing but added, "and please look after our boys—Amen." Our blue and white oil-cloth-covered table was filled with a country-style breakfast. There was thick, home-cured bacon, over-easy eggs cooked in the bacon grease, baking powder biscuits, and fresh from the tree, sliced Alberta peaches. Dad had already milked the cows and fed the horses. The family car was backed up to the yard gate for our twenty minute drive to the fruit shipping town of Parlier.

There had been little to pack, just basic toiletries. By the end of this day my civilian clothes would be packaged and sent home, courtesy of the army. All goodbyes had been said, and we talked about the farewell party two days before with all of Dad's family and many friends. Herb had called from the University of Redlands to say goodbye and to announce his promotion to first lieutenant. His parting advice was, "You'll take a lot of insults in boot camp bud,—You're not used to that—Just don't take it personally." I didn't know what that meant. I took everything personally, but I thanked him anyway.

As the sun continued to rise and brightened our kitchen, we all agreed that cooler weather was a welcome relief in the San Joaquin Valley. I found myself watching my parents very closely, as if to memorize their images. My Dad, a kind of Clark Gable look-alike, was not tall but was very muscular and the most natural, unaffected person I had ever known. He loved my mother passionately and cared about everybody. Herb and I were agreed that our Mom was the prettiest mother around. Very ladylike, but loved to be teased by her three men.

She single-handedly improved the quality of our life, the appearance of our ranch and home, and the manners of everyone under her roof. I could not imagine life without them. I next absorbed the kitchen, the vineyards, the big red barn with its surrounding corrals, the Sierras, the orange grove, the giant oak tree shading the tank house, and the eucalyptus trees lining the driveway from the road into our yard. I somehow knew that I would want these memories in the days ahead.

A warm closeness and camaraderie had always characterized our family of four, and I was very aware of it this morning. Also, Mom and Dad were very much in love and had a way of drawing even closer when facing a painful experience. It was clear that Mom was standing closer to Dad this morning as she poured him another cup of coffee. He leaned his head against her as he put an arm around her and said softly, "We're going to miss you, son. It will be very hard with both of you gone." We vowed to write often. Then, with a sudden twinkle in his eye, Dad asked, "So how was your date last night?"

"It was the best date I ever had," I responded happily. We were all relieved by the diversion as I poured out the details.

My good friend Wally and I had discovered a mutual interest in dating a very pretty girl named Margie from Dinuba. Since we were leaving for the service one day apart, we decided to go see her together before he left yesterday, leaving the competitive field even for later on. We had a great time together. She was amazing. So amazing I decided 'all is fair in love and war,' and went back to see her last night after seeing Wally off for the navy in the morning.

"Will there be any problem with Wally?" my dad asked gently.

"I'm not very worried about that, Dad. I don't think they really clicked very well and besides, I know he stopped in to see two other girls on his way home. And you know what? Margie seemed to get a kick out of it when I told her the story. She was a lot of fun and she was, uh,— really —uh, — very affectionate. She gave me a picture and said she'd write to me." My folks knew of Margie and liked her. Then Dad asked if I needed any money until I got my first paycheck. I thanked him and said I didn't. I had just been paid thirty dollars by the Skeleton Club for playing drums with a combo at their last three dances.

Then he said, "Son, you have a lot of ways to make a living after the war. Just don't be a farmer." Then it was time to go.

As we assembled at the car, Mom was having a hard time holding back tears, but began to hum a tune, which was often her way of controlling feelings. Once out the driveway we passed the large canal where I had slipped in at the age of four and been pulled out of the water by our first family dog, Curly. One mile up the road we passed my elementary school, where Herb and I both spent eight years. Dad had also gone to school there for a short time and Uncle Herman had always been on the board of directors, which never seemed to benefit me in any particular way. This was where I had been locked in a battle of wills for many years with the principal, Mrs. Bronte, who unfortunately had also been my teacher. There was the corner of the playground where many of us who had ridden our horses to school would congregate. We would keep them there until Mrs. Bronte would ring the bell to line up for school. Then we would tie the reins up over their necks and let them all go at the same time. They would take off on four different roads for home. Of course the only drawback to this was that we had to walk home after school.

As Parlier came into sight we could see that the bus had already arrived a little ahead of time. There appeared to be about four or five other guys my age with their families, waiting to board. We joined the group where Dad knew two of the fathers. Good-natured, stoic banter prevailed as the bus driver checked his watch. He was clearly reluctant to end the farewells being exchanged. "All aboard," he finally called and the families stepped back.

Dad and I shook hands vigorously and then broke the rules and embraced. In that instant, I knew the power of my father's love. It allowed me to feel the deep pain of loss and to also be able to survive it. In his embrace, and in all of his contact with me I felt his sincere, uncomplicated affection and appreciation of who I was. Mom's appreciation, also strong, had a little more to do with who I could become. Both of them wanted me to be safe, but Mom also wanted me to be a Lieutenant, like Herb.

As Mom and I hugged, her tears finally spilled over. Dad put his arms around both of us. I told her I loved her and would write often as I pulled away and became the last one to board the bus. A seat on the side where they were standing allowed me to wave goodbye as the driver shifted into gear, closed the door and drove off. His last words to the assembled families and friends were "Don't worry folks. I'll take good care of them." I tried hard to swallow my own tears as I looked back through the rear window and saw Mom and Dad standing there, arms around each other, fading into the distance.

Mom and Dad
Christmas, 1945

Mom and Dad

Surrogate

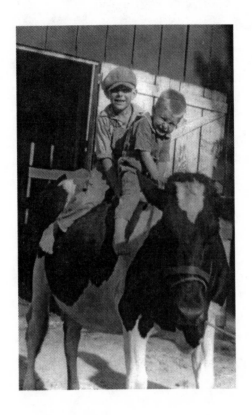

Horseplay with big brother

Grape Harvest

COLONEL KING'S MOB

On April 6th, we began fighting our way East toward Attendorn, rolling through four or five towns a day. The Germans would pull back through a couple of towns and then dig in for a fight. We were often the second wave, following our brother regiments, cleaning up pockets of resistance and rear-guard machine gun nests. We were slowed by roadblocks of tree trunks and rocks stacked on the road, that had to be blown away or pushed away by our supporting tanks. We sometimes walked between towns, especially if we were approaching one that was fortified for a fight. Truck convoys were sometimes available to carry us quickly to points of resistance manned by SS troops. Even as the second wave of assault, we were often under fire from snipers and lost German patrols separated from units that had been captured or had retreated. With several artillery and mortar battalions attached to us, and with our planes bombing or strafing, we struggled up to the outskirts of Attendorn.

We had usually managed to bed down late at night in some of the 'open' towns, where we took over homes and moved families into their cellars or limited portions of their homes. With one squad of twelve men to a dwelling, we had to take turns each night sleeping in the beds. I had never slept between thick, down-filled comforters before. Familiar sights in most homes were framed pictures of young soldiers with a wide black ribbon across one corner. Several couples who would see us staring at the pictures would quickly assure us that their sons were killed by Russians, not Americans. I thought about the inevitability of the day my folks would hang a gold star in our living room window to replace one of the two blue stars now proudly displayed. Ever since the first day of combat I felt I was living on borrowed time. German families in these situations seemed frightened at first, and then confused by the combination of our hostile aggressiveness and our youthfulness.

To our amazement, we often found running water, indoor flushing toilets, electric lights and cleanliness. Out of sight of their neighbors, many of the German women and children were actually friendly. We were not supposed to fraternize but we did anyway. The situation was different in demolished cities where the survivor citizens were understandably cold and hostile. We knew that they had little food, and for the most part did not take their food or commandeer food from stores.

Looting, though forbidden, was widespread. I did my share, but took only military souvenirs that I would find such as swords, pistols, helmets, rifles and medals. These were usually from prisoners. Some of my buddies were wrapping up silver sets, coin collections, rare books and jewelry to send home through Army mail as souvenirs. I reminded my squad of military regulations regarding looting and left it at that. I wanted no more enemies in combat. Keeping an eye on Brewster was bad enough. Word was out that Brewster had forced a young girl in one of the houses to have sex with him while he was on guard duty, and then gave her a lot of loot to keep quiet. The thought occurred to me that I might shoot him along the way, maybe in the thick of a fire-fight.

Following Colonel King, our Regiment stormed into the city of Attendorn on April 12th and relieved the attacking regiment. They had suffered heavy casualties. "What took you so long?" was the main taunt we heard as we moved through their ranks and advanced slowly through the town that had become the front line in bloody house-to-house fighting. Lieutenant Kramer, aware of my sniper training, called me up to a sheltered vantage point where snipers had pinned us down. I tossed Kramer my walkie- talkie and moved up shakey stairs to the second floor of a clothing store. A shell had torn off the roof but I found two corner windows with views of the small town square and looked out carefully, staying in the shadows of the room. Four members of our company were lying on the cobblestones. One was moving and moaning, the other three were still. We knew if we tried to help them we would be shot.

Familiar voices began shouting out locations and distances while I slowly searched likely high spots for the snipers. Then I saw the first one straight across the square from me in the shadows, aiming at the corner where Kramer was hiding. I set my sight for a hundred and fifty yards, threaded my left arm through my rifle strap to brace for a standing shot and aimed. Then to calm myself I took several long deep breaths, imagined I was on the rifle range, let out only half of the third breath and held it as I slowly squeezed the trigger keeping my sights lined up on a spot below the guy's helmet. I could hear my sniper trainer saying, "You should always be surprised when your rifle fires. If you know when it fires, it means you jerked the trigger and you will miss."

I must have done it right. I was surprised when my rifle fired and through my sight I saw the sniper fall into the street. His rifle and helmet clattered around on the street as I dropped quickly to the floor to escape the inevitable volley of bullets. None came. They must not have seen me standing in the shadows. Getting up slowly, I moved into the shadows of a different window just in case, this time needing to shoot from my left shoulder. Wishing I had a telescopic sight I promised myself that I would get that German Mauser with a top mounted telescope as soon as possible. I could 'zero it in' for use and then take it home to Uncle Vern as a souvenir. After a long period of quiet, Kramer decided we had to get moving. Half the platoon would charge the buildings across the square and the other half would give covering fire. "Keep your eyes peeled, Andy," he yelled as he led the charge. Two snipers emerged immediately and wounded two more of our guys. I picked off one and somebody else got the third one. No one else was in these buildings so I picked up the best of the Mauser sniper rifles, slung it over my shoulder and rejoined my platoon. Now I had my telescopic sight. Marty and another medic began treating the wounded men.

We moved on up the street where the retreating Krauts would be waiting for us. Without holes to dive into when they fired at us we leap-frogged with another squad from building to building, jumping over bodies from yesterday's battle up the same street As usual in these circumstances, my impacted wisdom tooth was aching and swelling. I also had to remind myself to keep an eye on corporal Brewster who had threatened to "get me." Luckily, he was nowhere to be seen and I was staying close to Lt. Kramer with a walkie-talkie. Unfortunately, Kramer liked to be right out in front.

I learned that constantly moving on the attack was safer than pausing in doorways. I discovered this as I paused in the doorway of a leather shop to catch my breath. I kicked in the door and found a store full of leather gun cases and pistol holsters. I grabbed a double shoulder holster from a large stack and strapped it on. Then I noticed a terrified woman huddled with her young son in the far corner of the room. I quickly held up a calming hand saying, "It's O.K., It's O.K." assuming that this was universally understood. Then I tossed her a wad of German money I had taken from some prisoners. She said, "Danke, Danke" many times and somehow let me know this was not her store. She had run inside it when the shooting started. It was owned by a Nazi who had left with the retreating army. I took my German Luger and P-38 out of my field jacket pockets and slipped them into the holsters as I said goodbye. When I stepped out onto the porch again, a bullet or shrapnel creased my hip, and I could feel blood running down my leg as I sprinted out into the street and kept running. *No more pauses for me*, I thought as I caught up with the rest of my unit.

The few remaining Germans were busy surrendering when we heard cheering and discovered that we had arrived at a huge labor camp containing thousands of Russian and Polish prisoners. They had already captured the camp commandant and several guards and were parading them through the streets of the camp and into one of the prisoner cages. The POWs poured out into the town as we tore down the gates and fences. Many of the prisoners were immediately on the roads leading out of town to the west. Some scoured the cities, collapsed buildings and basements, looking for guards and SS troops that might be hiding, beating them to death when they found them.

We drew back into the town for the night, leaving outposts at the perimeter and found some of the men we had relieved. The wound on my hip was stinging, but the bleeding had stopped and I decided to keep an eye out for an Aid Station. Suddenly, we saw the sky light up on the outskirts where we had just been. The Germans were laying down a barrage of white phosphorous shells on our former position. We all squirmed as we recalled the way phosphorous can burn all the way to the bone if it touches you.

Coincidentally at that moment we noticed the smell of meat cooking. Rounding a corner we came upon a complete beef carcass being rotated over an open fire on a metal fence post. I asked where they got the cow and a corporal explained, "Well, we found it in a back yard but our C.O. told us we couldn't steal food from the enemy. So what we did was, we had ourselves a court-martial and found this here cow guilty of giving milk to the enemy and decided execution was the appropriate sentence for treason. You guys want to stay for dinner?"

Jerry said, "Damn right we're staying. We haven't seen our mess truck for days. What time are you serving?"

"Looks like it ought'a cook for another hour or so. Glad to have you join us. Say Andy, what's the matter with your jaw —it's all swollen?"

I said, "It's an impacted wisdom tooth. It swells up everytime we attack. Know where the Aid Station is?" The corporal said it was close by and gave us directions.

Jerry said, "Come on Andy, I'll go with you. They can take a look at your hip at the same time."

The Aid Station was actually a field hospital set up in an office building on the main street. A field Doc looked at my leg, cleaned the laceration, sprinkled sulfa powder on it and taped a bandage over it saying, "Just a scratch, you got off lucky. You sure that's the only wound? That's a lot of blood on your pants." We looked and found four more pieces of shrapnel in my leg.

As he dismissed us, Jerry said, "Hey, doesn't this rate a purple heart?"

The Doc snorted, "Hell no. These are all superficial. You gotta be disabled. But get over to the dentist there. That tooth might rate you one. That looks real bad. Must hurt like hell."

The dentist was the same drunken idiot I had gone to in Cologne. Now he stood waiting for me eagerly with a foot-powered field drill in his hand attached to a pedal stand operated by a very young assistant.

He looked in my mouth and snorted in exasperation. "You have an impacted wisdom tooth. Why didn't you come in sooner? Have you been grinding your teeth?"

"Yes," I said, "But only when I'm being shot at."

"Well, I can't do anything until the swelling goes down," he added.

"I did come in when it wasn't swollen and you sent me away. Don't you remember?"

He laid down his drill in disgust. "Why should I remember you? You guys all look alike when you come in here. Come back when it's not swollen," he slurred.

"If I do, you'll just tell me I'm faking." He looked away as he waved me to the door, at which point I boiled over. "If you don't know what the hell you're doing, you better get a dentist in here who does, you god-damned drunken idiot."

His face was now purple with rage as he spun around screaming, "Get the hell out of here, Corporal. I'm reporting you for insubordination."

"Lots of luck, Jerk. You don't even know who I am. We all look alike, remember?"

Following me out of the building, the young assistant, a PFC, handed me a bag full of ice and told me it would help reduce the swelling. "He can't help it. He drinks a lot, you know. God, that tooth must hurt. Maybe you can stop grinding your teeth." The ice bag did help, as I stumbled my way back to the beef dinner, wondering how I could possibly chew on anything.

Jerry joined me as I walked out and I asked if he heard what went on. He had and said we'd probably do better with a German dentist. I detoured into the dentist's living quarters and when I came out Jerry asked where I went. I said, "Oh, I found his whiskey bottle and took a piss in it." With my spirits lifted we soon greeted our hosts at the bar-b-que.

While sitting around the fire, chewing on very tough beef, Jerry leaned over to me and asked, "Andy, where the hell did you get that shoulder holster. I want one too." I told him about the leather store and said we could stop there on our way back.

It was beginning to get dark, so we headed through the rubble to our company area. I had used my scarf around my head to hold the ice bag on my jaw and the swelling was going down. We went directly to the leather store where we each loaded up with about twenty-five shoulder holsters each, and then proceeded up the street in an icy drizzle. I was pleased that we had stolen them from a Nazi. Jerry, being more cynical, doubted the woman's story. He figured she was the guy's wife and probably a Nazi too.

My communication squad had taken over a large home with many bedrooms and the radio had been brought inside where it was squawking out messages in code. Furniture had been broken up to make a large warm fire in a massive fireplace. My buddies were sitting around eating 'C' rations, so Jerry and I decided it would be generous not to tell them about our fresh meat dinner. Instead we threw the holsters on the floor and they each grabbed one. The word spread and soon everyone in the company of about fifty men had strapped on a brand new shoulder holster. Jerry and I had set aside one special hand-tooled work of art for Colonel King.

At one point, a jeep arrived with a couple of cases of wine from a winery that Company 'E' had captured. With radio messages assuring us that the enemy was quiet tonight, the party began. As a non-drinker, I had never tasted red wine before and found it rather nice. About an hour later everyone was very happy and we sang every drinking song and round that we knew.

Later, while writing down a message letter by letter, I slowly grasped the meaning and yelled at everybody to "Knock it off." With my chest tightening, I asked Sergeant Sherman at Regimental Headquarters to switch to voice and to repeat the message.

Into the stunned silence, the speaker voice crackled, "Word received from Eisenhower's Supreme Command that our President, Franklin D. Roosevelt died today and that the Vice President, Harry S. Truman was sworn in as President."

The silence was finally broken by Jerry who said, "Oh, shit! I don't need this! He was the best we ever had. We probably would have starved if he hadn't created the W.P.A." Few of us had heard of Harry Truman.

It was as if we had suddenly become fatherless and were lost in the wilds of hell. During the night, the poison injected into the bottles of wine by retreating Germans began to take effect. Within hours we were all ill and convulsing. I was as sick as I had been in the hospital at Le Havre. Another company that had been spared the gift of wine, moved over to protect us while we recovered. A couple of men who drank a lot of it died from the poison which turned out to be buzz-bomb fuel.

Colonel King looked in on us with words of comfort. Still weak from vomiting for about eight hours, Jerry and I handed him his special shoulder holster. He immediately strapped it on and filled it with two army 45s. He said, "I know you paid for this, so I'll accept it with thanks." Pausing at the door he turned and announced, "You'll have to be well tomorrow. We have to take Herscheid away from the SS. We ought'a scare the hell out'a them. We look like a bunch of gangsters."

THE GATES OF HELL

As we approached Herscheid on April 15th we could see that no white flags were flying and the sky at dusk became ominous with large, dark rain clouds. Thunder, lightning and icy rain cast a forbidding gloom over the town and then seemed to be reaching out for us a mile away. Jerry saw me staring at the main entrance to the city surrounded with sand-bagged machine gun bunkers and asked, "What do you think, Andy?"

"Looks like the gates of hell," I responded. Intelligence and Reconnaissance had reported that the Germans were still in the town and had been reinforced. They had stopped running. We poured out of our trucks and spread out into the fields with three battalions abreast. Then at a fast walk we moved forward in a single line.

Lightning flashes were joined by artillery and mortar flashes, as the shells came pouring in on us. Soon there were lots of shell holes which provided a good beginning for foxholes. We were ordered to dig-in, as shells from our rear began to bombard the city and surrounding area. The screams for medics were everywhere and could be heard throughout the night as the shelling continued. My walkie-talkie squawked out a message that the Germans were counter-attacking with Tiger tanks. Bazooka teams were moving up to join us on the front line. Grenade launchers which fitted on the muzzles of M1s were made ready and fitted with anti-tank grenades.

After many hours of shelling and with icy rain pouring into my crater, I had the feeling for the first time that I couldn't take anymore. I could see why guys would crack. No one in my squad had been hit yet, but I couldn't believe we would escape death much longer. I felt very alone as we had spaced ourselves out so one shell wouldn't get so many of us, about fifteen feet apart. Then it happened. A large mortar round, which we heard coming, hit Josh's crater and his pulverized body came down on us with the rain. His helmet and rifle were implanted in the hole but Josh was gone. His best friend Bennie was crying and vomiting while moaning, "God-damn bastards," over and over. I knew it would be hard to tell Josh's family that there was nothing left of him to bury. I would not tell them how he was with us for the attack at daybreak. We could hear the tanks in the distance. They would come at us at dawn.

I spent the rest of the night in my foxhole, scraping Josh off of my clothes with my trench knife, and trying to control my nausea by reliving every intimate moment with my high school girlfriends, my last furlough with Margie and my last night with Danielle in the LeHarve hospital. Thinking of my folks helped quiet my fear and renewed my sense of purpose. I wanted to believe I was saving them all from this. I pushed aside the insistent image of Mom and Dad hanging up the gold star after reading the telegram and instead, imagined myself sitting at the kitchen table after the war, teasing Dad about his philosophy that every chore could be made into a fun game. That worked with cutting peaches, picking grapes, herding cattle, painting fences, plowing and irrigating, but not this.

During the night, word was relayed that a tank group would lead our attack on Herscheid in the morning. This would be the first time we would follow tanks into combat. A cheer went up just before dawn as a column of Sherman tanks thundered and clanked past us and began lobbing cannon shells into the city. At the same time, our artillery stepped up bombardment and Air Force planes bombed and fired rockets at the German tanks. I felt we had been saved, but our relief was short-lived. The two lead tanks were disabled and in flames, blocking the road into the city. Almost immediately, the order came over the backpack radio I was now carrying that we were to storm the city ahead of the tanks. After all of our practice in training on how to follow tanks and use them for protection, we were now to protect them. I still hadn't realized that our tanks were much more 'thin-skinned' than theirs'. I wondered why Colonel King hadn't done something to save us.

We moved out in attack formation. The field between the city and us filled with evenly spaced lines of troops followed by more lines of troops. The isolated feeling of the night disappeared, even without the tanks. The chaos of combat erupted. The sound of artillery going both ways overhead was soon overpowered by rifle and machine gun fire. Everyone was now zigzagging. Like the machine guns, we were running in short bursts. I would run for about five paces, empty my clip of eight rounds and then dive into the lowest spot available. Men began falling and medics were soon at their sides. One medic crumpled and died on top of the man he was helping. I saw Woody Foster from the I and R squad get hit in the stomach and fold up like a jackknife, as blood gushed from his mouth. Even with the bullets and shrapnel flying, it seemed wrong not to stop and help him, but we kept running. The city was in flames, thanks to our artillery and air force bombs. The SS counterattack had been stopped before it started, but resistance was fierce.

On the outskirts of the city we found ourselves pinned down. It was suicidal to think of standing up again. We re-formed our lines by squads, by crawling on our stomachs with weapons cradled in our arms, hugging the ground. Even the medics were unable to reach the increasing number of wounded. Few of us were below ground level and we knew our time was running out. I didn't dare to move to reach my shovel. The weight of the radio on my back was comforting. It felt like protection, and kept me flat.

Just then a jeep came roaring up the road with our battalion commander, Colonel King, standing up in the passenger side, holding on with one hand and pumping his arm and fist up and down, the infantry signal for attack. Even more surprising was the long, bright red scarf around his neck and flapping behind him. "Look alive!" he was shouting as he sped past us. "Let's go get 'em!" Without hesitation we were all on our feet following the speeding, weaving jeep as we swarmed into Herscheid, weathering the worst barrages of gunfire we had ever experienced. Colonel King seemed to be everywhere in his bright red scarf .

The bazooka teams, our most mobile infantry weapon against tanks, spread out looking for any remaining Tiger tanks. My job as a radio operator was to stay as close as possible to the company commander, Captain Sullivan, while shooting and ducking at the same time. At one point he crawled over to me to use the handset of the radio and found that a fifty-caliber bullet had gone through the radio, missing my body by about two inches. He went looking for another radio operator as I happily tossed mine into a cellar. I was now thirty pounds lighter. Then I noticed that my jaw was swollen and throbbing. My clenched teeth had caused another flair-up of my impacted wisdom teeth. The pain was excruciating. A medic came over to me thinking that I had been shot in the jaw and I didn't even try to stop him as he gave me a shot of morphine right in my neck. The pain eased instantly. When the order came from Sullivan to "Move out," I yelled, "Let's go get 'em."

Jerry said, "Jesus Christ, Andy you sound drunk. What the hell happened?" There was no time to explain.

We moved through the curving streets of the city, one house at a time. Tully Jackson, the assistant squad leader, caught a bullet through his hand that also went into his thigh. His was the only injury in my squad. We made him wait in an alley for a medic. We always became more aggressive and eager to retaliate whenever someone close to us was killed or injured. Civilians had been warned to leave, but many stayed and many died. We rescued some from collapsed buildings while dodging fire from slowly retreating Germans. We heard the sound of heavy fighting going on in another part of the city, about where I thought Company 'E' would be. By mid-day we had captured the town, taken two thousand prisoners, and left many dead on both sides. The grave detail would have a busy day tomorrow. By the time we re-grouped at the other end of town we were all wearing brightly colored scarves. The house-to-house searching had obviously been for more than German soldiers this time. I had found and was wearing a strip of brilliant orange negligee. Now high on morphine, I didn't really give a damn about much of anything. Thinking that I might not be as alert as I should be, I told Jerry the story and asked him to keep an eye on me. Making ourselves such good targets seemed to speed up our adrenaline and courage. The disciplined and rule-bound Germans were curiously intimidated by this show of recklessness. Prisoners reported thinking we were madmen, out of control and with no fear of death. On hearing this, we simply grinned and nodded.

My squad was asked to take our prisoners, numbering about a hundred, to a cage three streets away. We knew this would be some kind of a heavy wire fence stockade put up by engineers. Lt. Kramer gave me a rough sketch of the location and I led the column in a jeep, with Jerry manning a thirty-caliber machine gun. The rest of the squad divided up on each side of the prisoners who were content to do whatever we asked of them. After turning them over to the MPs at the cage, I noticed a red cross flag flying over an aid station and drove over to get some bandages for our shrapnel wounds.

As I walked into a kind of warehouse, the smell of ether and a chorus of, "Hey, Andy's" greeted me. About forty-five of my friends from Company 'E' were scattered around the wood floor on blankets. The dimly lit room looked like another battleground. Many of the guys, some of them from basic training and my time in the company, were badly wounded. Everyone who was conscious was high on morphine. I felt right at home. Marty and many other medics were moving quickly from one injured man to another. They would soon be on ambulance trucks to rear-area hospitals. Tom Quinn greeted me cheerfully with the good news that he was going home. A bullet had gone through his spinal cord. James McGregor, also on morphine, had a huge gaping hole in his thigh. I learned that many in the company had been killed. They had borne the brunt of a counterattack on our right flank. They had been told that our company had been wiped out. Tom figured they had lost about half of their company. Some of the guys asked what happened with my swollen jaw and neck. Feeling guilty in the midst of my wounded friends, I just shrugged it off with, "Ah, it's nothing." Along with the good-byes, Jerry and I were given some hastily written letters to mail for them.

A supply truck brought us ammunition, mail and a change of clothes on a first-come, first-serve basis. My squad, by mutual agreement, rolled up our discarded combat fatigues with the remnants of Josh on them and buried them in the little cemetery near our bivouac area. Ben left a note of explanation in the trigger guard of a rifle he stuck in the ground as a marker. I wondered how the grave detail would handle this one. A replacement radio arrived, and the first message I received for Lt. Kramer was an order to move north toward Hagan in one hour. Everyone had dug slit trenches hoping for some rest and the news was met with loud groans, until we heard that it was Colonel King who wanted to keep at the Germans before they had a chance to dig in. In spite of his admiration for our Colonel, Jerry quipped, "That son-of-a-bitch is determined to get us killed." We had not yet linked up with the 1st and 3rd Armies to close the trap. We were also running low on food. I couldn't remember the last hot meal.

With my trench knife I sliced open a 'K' ration and laid out the contents. With my two-inch, hinged can opener, nicknamed a 'P-38,' I opened a can of Spam and gobbled it down with three stale crackers and a Hershey chocolate bar. It was so cold I smoked one of the cigarettes just for the warmth. It was my first since I was nine years old. I usually used my Zippo lighter to warm my hands, but with this meal I used it to light a can of Sterno, to heat water in my canteen cup. I added the packet of Nescafe always found at the bottom of a 'K' ration and had a cup of coffee. I noticed that I only had two meals left and found it was the same for others in my platoon. Were we going to run out of food? Then the whistles sounded and we were loading on trucks, jeeps, and half-tracks, and moving north.

My Jeep

Herschied, Germany

Squad attacking village;
Rhur Valley in the rain

In the Black Forest;
Ruhr Valleuy, Germany

TRAPPED

For several days we advanced through the northern part of the Black Forest. Most of the fighting now was in the forest and between the cities. Many of the trees were stripped of leaves and branches and stood like wooden skeletons, victims of artillery, mortar, machine gun and rifle fire. We moved so fast that we outdistanced the divisions on both our left and right flanks. We had charged into the midst of a large German force and saw gunfire coming at us from all sides, including our rear. The Germans had counterattacked, slipped through the voids on our left and right and surrounded us. In the confusion the shooting stopped because we were running into each other and afraid to shoot for fear of hitting our own men.

We were all now trapped in the pocket together, and miniature pockets developed everywhere. My squad happened upon a German squad of five who immediately surrendered. Five minutes later two squads of Germans captured us and released our prisoners. As we were being herded together in great confusion, Lt. Kramer arrived with the rest of our platoon and our captors threw down their arms. In the dark of night our two guards went to sleep and our prisoners escaped into the forest. By shouting out passwords during the night, our company and finally our battalion drew together and established a perimeter of defense, like a large hole in a doughnut. After winning every battle for a week, we now faced the prospect of annihilation or being taken prisoner again. We expanded our circle to a diameter of several miles. They fought back with counterattacks. Then the shooting stopped on both sides and we dug in for a long wait. We did not really know how to fight a defensive war. I felt a new appreciation of my Uncle Ernest in the trenches of World War I . How does one go about surrendering—or do we fight to the death? If I asked him how to do this he would probably say, "Just be patient, and keep your head down. There's no hurry to get killed." I thought of digging a very deep hole and hiding until it was all over. Our food was gone, so I assumed the Germans were just going to starve us out. On the other side of the Germans were our 1st and 3rd Armies. We were caught with our enemy in the same trap.

We sent out patrols and so did they. Now everyone tried to avoid shooting. We knew the Germans couldn't get out of this pocket and they probably wanted to give up, but they kept fighting anyway. Cold rain, fog and the darkness of the forest increased the tension, as did our increasing hunger. For two days we had been without food when things took a very sinister turn. While on patrol, my squad captured a small camp, where one of our missing patrols was imprisoned in a compound. We discovered that some of our men had fingers and toes shot off for each article of German equipment they had in their possession. In our fury we gave the German squad a choice. Either let our butchered guys even the score or be killed immediately. Our guys, though weak from loss of blood, took turns and shot off toes and fingers from those that had done it to them. Then we let them go, not wanting to have to explain all of this.

At this point, the battle in the Ruhr Pocket, as it became known, became personal and bitter. Our rescued wounded could not be evacuated, so they simply rejoined their squads, heavily bandaged by our medics. When we discovered that this practice by the Germans was continuing, we began to apply the same rule to other prisoners. Carrying a Thompson sub-machine gun? You lose a finger. Our own victims of this butchery were often first in line to administer retaliatory justice. I know that I wasn't the only one to hide my souvenirs on the mess truck and to begin carrying only government-issued equipment. We kept our scarves, but our supply truck filled up quickly with German weapons of every kind, including my beloved burp gun and my shoulder-holstered Luger pistols.

I had never really experienced hunger before and I imagined that was why people would sometimes surrender. The gnawing feeling in my stomach could be eased by drinking lots of plentiful rainwater. My company was scattered around on one farm complex, mostly inside barns and outbuildings to escape the periodic rains. Eric and his 2nd squad had taken over the basement of the farm house and my squad was enjoying the luxury of a haystack in one of the barns. Somebody noticed smoke pouring from a basement window under the house and some of us went to investigate. We found Eric and several other men crouched around wood fires burning under three steel helmets hanging on wires from the ceiling. The helmets were full of boiling oil borrowed from the kitchen upstairs and everyone was furiously peeling potatoes stored in a large pile in the corner. Then the potatoes were cut in long slim strips placed in squares of helmet netting and dropped into the boiling oil. French fries had never sounded so good. A line soon formed as men lined up to peel and French fry a potato. We even gave some to the farm couple confined to their kitchen and bedroom. They gave us some bottles of wine in return, which our replacements drank. They had not been with us when we nearly died on wine that had been injected with rocket fuel.

A new replacement said he had seen deer in the forest nearby. We borrowed a jeep with a thirty-caliber machine gun mounted on the back, and went hunting for either Germans or a deer, whichever came first. We found a thicket of brush which proved to be a perfect place to wait. When a large buck appeared, a short burst of three bullets brought him down. Back at the farm house, Charley, a butcher's son, quickly skinned, cleaned and prepared the deer for roasting in the basement, where the fire could not be seen so clearly. No one could remember their last meal of fresh food.

Suddenly, three jeeps came storming into our farm yard. The flowing red scarf in the first jeep told us Colonel King was paying a visit. His radio operator had heard that our headquarters company was eating venison. We crowded around his jeep as he pulled two bottles of bourbon from under his seat and jumped down with a big grin on his weather-beaten face. He said, in his usual commanding tone, "A good guest always brings something for dinner." We led him to the basement and served him a mess-kit full of venison and French fries. The bottles of bourbon were gone almost instantly.

He shook hands with Captain Sullivan, our reserved company commander, who wore no scarf and said with a grin, "I'm glad there's somebody in this outfit who knows how to dress properly." Then scanning all our negligee scarves he added, "A lot of women must be sleeping naked in this neck of the woods." When he heard that I was the one who shot the deer with a machine gun, he walked up to me for a good look. "I'll be God-damned," he said cuffing me on the shoulder. "You're the guy I promoted to Corporal in a court-martial. Then you get me this shoulder holster and now you bring home fresh meat. Jesus Christ, why aren't you on my staff?" Then he hopped in his jeep and drove off alone. As he sped off he shouted that help was on the way and that we were going to break out of the pocket soon. Later, with full stomach, soft bed of hay, the bourbon and distant, rolling gunfire I lapsed into a full night of sleep. The first in two weeks.

The roar of planes flying low brought us outside as morning light forced its way through our perpetual heavy mist. We waited for the chattering sound of machine guns on a strafing run. Instead, the sky was filled with parachutes, which scared the hell out of us until we identified the planes as our own C-47 cargo planes. Parachutes were attached to large containers of food. They were opened as quickly as they landed, and were filled with boxes labeled '10-in-1 Rations.' We had heard about these 'gourmet' meals where one box would feed 10 men. Everyone was stuffing their back packs with canned raw bacon, cans of fruit, custards, small cakes, other kinds of canned meat, candy and cigarettes. We also loaded up with bandoleers of ammunition and distributed some of the replacement rifles and machine guns that had also been dropped. Even bags of mail had been dropped to us, which created more excitement than the food. As Chester handed out the mail, I received a large packet of letters while many of the men received nothing. I quickly shoved them into my pocket to ease my embarrassment and focused on a package from home. A box of cookies had turned to dust. I quickly served up the cookie dust in the little wax paper cups, while another fortunate guy handed out salami slices.

The smell of the venison of the night before had yielded to the aroma of bacon, hanging in strips from sticks over open fires. The eating frenzy halted abruptly as an order came from Regimental Headquarters to prepare for another attack. This time to try to break out of our trap. Patrols were sent out in all directions to find the weakest point in the German defense. I went with Marty as radioman to send back information and we found Colonel King, unconscious at the wheel of his jeep where it had crashed against a tree. His scalp had almost been ripped off by a wire still stretched across the road at head height. Blood was everywhere and still pouring out of his head. The wire, probably rigged by the kids in the Hitler-Jugend, had been well placed and slipped under King's helmet. Marty quickly opened his field kit and sprinkled sulfa powder on the raw flesh. He threaded two needles with olive drab thread and handed me one.

"Thank God he's almost bald," Marty said, "Or we'd have to shave him. Just pretend you're sewing up a rip in your blanket, Andy," he instructed. We each took a side, starting at the back and met at the front. Just when this morning's breakfast seemed about to come up, Marty announced cheerfully, "How about this? We just saved our Colonel's scalp."

I said, "I sure hope so 'cause he sure saved mine once." Then we wiped off all the matted blood we could, dabbed antiseptic on the stitches and wrapped his head in yards of gauze. King awakened just as we finished. A large knot had grown on his forehead from the crash. We moved him from his steaming jeep into ours and explained what had happened as we drove him back to our aid station. He was incredulous at first, but when he saw all the blood on his uniform he said, "I guess some serious thanks are in order. God, what headache." At the Aid station he got out, said thanks again, and went into a tent muttering, "I don't have time for this." As he disappeared, Marty shouted to a medic, "He got that in combat. Make sure they know he's eligible for a purple heart." Back in the barn that night I realized that it was April 17th. Tomorrow would be my 20th birthday. Tomorrow we would breakout. Would I be killed on my birthday?

Next morning, as we prepared for our attack to the north, a crackling order came into my radio jeep to hold our position instead. An entire armored division was coming to our rescue. We cheered as we heard the tanks approaching. When they came into view, the commander of the lead tank was standing in the turret.

Jerry said, "I'll be damned, that looks like Patton himself."

I answered, "I'm not sure, Jerry, but look who's standing beside him."

It was our Colonel King, with red scarf flying and a bloody bandage on his head pumping his arm up and down, shouting, "Let's get the hell out of this hell hole." Our vehicles fell into line between the Shermans, and the men on foot were pulled aboard the tanks by men already there. We sliced through the encirclement and proceeded to cut the pocket into quarters.

As the 1st and 3rd Armies closed in with tanks in the lead, the entire Northern German Army of over three hundred thousand Wehrmacht and SS troops were captured along with all their equipment and vehicles. Small pockets of fighting erupted briefly until the word of the Rhur collapse reached everyone. Germans were pouring out of the forest and jamming the roads as they tried to find a place to surrender without being killed. They were assembled in huge open fields and we found ourselves serving as human cages around various units, just to keep them from drifting away. They were searched but left with most of their personal effects. Many were actually smiling and eager to tell us how glad they were to be out of the war. In one pile of belongings taken from the prisoners I found a sparkling silver pendant with beautiful stones on a silver chain. I scooped it up, knowing this would be the gift I wanted to send to Danielle. SS troops were kept separate and were usually sullen. It was clear that the Wehrmacht soldiers hated them. We stocked up on pistols, Nazi emblems, Iron Crosses, and daggers.

I busied myself for a while, packaging up the souvenirs and wrote a letter to Danielle. I let her know that I was still alive and thanked her for her care in the hospital, for our last night together and for her help in getting me back to the 86th. I enclosed the necklace. Then, I handed the letter and the box of trophies over to a clerk on the mail truck, wondering if it would ever get to their destinations. Jerry came over and with his crooked grin in place, handed me a tiny, pearl-handled

Beretta pocket pistol he had taken from a German officer and said, "Happy Birthday Andy. It's April the 18th, and you're still alive."

The mail truck had brought more mail and as often happened after mail-call, news from home was shouted out for any one who might be interested. At one point Lieutenant Kramer walked up with a newspaper clipping saying, "I think you guys ought to hear this." He then read that the former members of the Army Specialized Training Program, trained at Fort Benning, Georgia were distinguishing themselves in front-line combat divisions in Europe instead of in college. He read on that a large proportion of the 86th Blackhawk division was made up of A.S.T.P.ers.

Jerry immediately quipped, "Is that supposed to make us feel good? I'm supposed to be studying Engineering at Columbia University. Where were you headed Andy?"

"Engineering at Berkeley. But look at it this way, Jerry. Where else could we have learned how to use P-38 can-openers." As Kramer sauntered off, a little crestfallen, it was clear to me that we all shared a lingering feeling of betrayal. We all wanted to fight but we had been cheated out of the earlier choices of service by qualifying for A.S.T.P. While trying to distract myself by cleaning my new Beretta pistol, Jerry came over and confided that it had belonged to a woman officer.

A.S.T.P.

It came without warning. There weren't even rumors leading up to the devastating news delivered to us by our training commander at the Infantry School in Fort Benning, Georgia. But there we were, in an unexpected Saturday morning formation in front of our barracks. Spirits had been soaring the night before. After four months of training in an Army Specialized Training Program boot camp, we were to be given our assignments to colleges and universities all over the country. Commissions as second lieutenants were to follow. I was to study electrical engineering at the University of California in Berkeley. I waited in line three hours to phone my folks with the good news. We would all return to our home states. Most of us were up all night exchanging addresses and celebrating, so the early morning formation found most of us pretty groggy.

Colonel Bradford, speaking to the entire battalion over a small PA system, was solemn and shaken as he said he had some very bad news for us. Our training corporals and sergeants, all veterans of the African Campaign, flanked him on both sides looking equally gloomy. Behind them the early morning sun was shining through the jump towers of the neighboring paratroop school. Sounds of armored division tanks warming up at the cavalry school drifted in from behind us. The Colonel, holding a War Department communiqué, announced that due to the urgent need for ground troops, the entire A.S.T.P. program was to be disbanded immediately and trainees were to be assigned to various combat units for service in Europe and the South Pacific. In the brief, stunned silence he added, "Boys, you won't be going to college. At least not now. You'll be assigned to three different infantry divisions for further combat training and then you'll head overseas."

A roar of protest exploded. "Not fair! How stupid can they be? What a chicken shit outfit. Send the War Department to the front."

"Fubar--Fubar--Fubar," was chanted in unison, meaning our situation was 'fucked up beyond all recognition.'

Above the protests, the Colonel added, "I know how disappointed you are and I want you to know that your training record was the highest of any group we've had. Maybe it will help to know that you're not alone. Many men in Air Corps flight training, Signal Corps and Paratroop jump school are being pulled out of their programs and sent to combat units. A.S.T.P.'ers already in college are being reassigned."

The Colonel allowed the protesting briefly but then called us to attention. Obediently, we snapped-to as he delivered the rest of the bad news. "Any requests for transfers into any other branch of the service or specialty will not be accepted. Also, there will be no weekend passes. The staff has decided that everyone will need a couple of days to cool down and get adjusted to this change." Another roar of protest went up as the Colonel turned us over to our company commanders. It was hard to get so much bad news from someone I respected so much. Colonel Bradford wore three rows of ribbons, had three purple hearts and had led combat teams in North Africa, Italy and on D-Day. In the meantime, we were restricted to the base. I knew it was because they were afraid we would tear up the nearby city of Columbus. It occurred to me that there might be another reason for restricting us to the camp. It would be harder for guys to go A.W.O.L. After telling us that our new assignments would be posted on Monday morning, Lt. Madsen dismissed us.

Best friends fell into groups immediately as we walked slowly back to our barracks on the packed white sand of our company street. My head was spinning and I just wanted to lie down on my bunk. Jerry sat down on my footlocker saying, "Well, when the army screws you it sure does a good job." J.C. and Tully sat on my bunk as we tried to adjust to what had just happened. We felt duped and betrayed. None of us would have deliberately signed up for the Army Infantry. We all had other interests and skills that would have been welcomed in other services. We were here because we received high scores on a special IQ test given when we were seniors in high school. We had passed up opportunities to enlist in other specialized services with the promise of an O.C.S. type of basic training, then into a college or university. Commissions would follow if we did well. After all of that we were now going to be foot solders with the lowly rank of buck private.

I was a ham radio operator. I could have been in the Signal Corps. In the Monterey reception center I had been assigned as a drummer to the Presidio military band and also the dance band. That could have been permanent. In complete disbelief, the band director accepted my preference to go with the A.S.T.P. assignment at Fort Benning. Tully had a private pilot's license and Jerry spoke three languages. J.C. had passed up straight infantry O.C.S.. Even though we were bitterly disappointed and really scared at the prospect of being thrown into a depleted infantry division as replacements, we wanted somehow to trust that the War Department knew what it was doing and that we must really be in trouble overseas. Someone across the barracks quipped, "It would be just our luck to be assigned to Patton."

"Don't rush to the phones at the PX," someone warned. "There's a line a mile long." I had thought of running to the phone earlier, but I felt too queasy and I wanted to get my perspective clear before I talked to my folks. Just yesterday I had shared the good news with them. Now this. I would wait. I knew they would be upset and I wanted to sound calm.

At this same moment, my folks were hearing about the cancellation of our program on a news broadcast and were worried about how I would be taking it. Although alcohol was forbidden in the barracks, a lot of whisky bottles appeared. Some of the guys were just sitting on their bunks staring at the floor, looking more and more depressed. About half of the two rows of double deck bunks were occupied by guys furiously writing letters. I was aware of a gnawing feeling of failure. J.C. hit it on the head when he commiserated with, "God, Andy, now I know how guys feel when they wash-out of flight training." Helpless rage seethed through our fifty-man barracks as we each tried to take back some sense of control over our lives.

Two hundred and fifty-pound Woody Kendrick yelled, "Fucking Shit!" and threw his footlocker through a window and ran outside. We never saw him again.

On Sunday morning we learned that about twenty guys in our battalion were AWOL, including Kendrick. A guy in the next barracks had too much to drink and tried to hang himself with his rifle sling in the middle of the night. Luckily, someone had come into the latrine to pee and cut him down in time. We also found the assignment list posted ahead of schedule. Our entire barracks had been assigned to the 86th Blackhawk Infantry Division stationed at Camp Livingston, near Alexandria, Louisiana. A brief history of the unit indicated that it had functioned in World War I and again now, as a training Division to supply replacements to combat units overseas. Just officers and non-coms were left. We would be leaving by train the next day, Monday.

J.C. and I took a long walk around our camp to share our misery. We bought things we didn't need at the PX and took in a matinee at the camp theater, a war film with Clark Gable. While talking about Louisiana, J.C. suddenly asked, "Andy, do you know much about the South?" I said I didn't although I was distantly related to Robert E. Lee. He said, "You know, it's a lot different than we're used to. There are separate buses, toilets and water fountains for blacks and whites." I was shocked. He said even restaurants and stores are separated. "God knows what our officers and non-coms will be like, especially if they were raised in the South. We could be in for some trouble." I didn't know what he was talking about. It seemed really dumb but J.C. was very smart and had traveled a lot, so I figured there was probably something to worry about. As for the officers, I comforted myself with the thought that we would at least out-number them.

We agreed that we would not miss Columbus, the only accessible town for day-passes. We were restricted to camp or barracks most week-ends during training and on the three times we did get passes we found it wasn't worth the long bus trip. The streets were jammed with Fort Benning trainees from the jump school and the Cavalry tank school. The best entertainment was a crowded movie theater or watching the frequent fights between paratroopers and tank jockeys. Women were understandably aloof and in short supply. Newly crowned second lieutenants from the Officer's Candidate School were everywhere, returning the required salutes from thousands of enlisted men roaming the main streets. Whenever we were in a group of buddies we would sometimes walk single file so officers would have to salute each one of us, especially if they had their arm around a woman.

By the time I reached my folks by phone that night I had packed my duffel bag and had dinner in the mess hall. The cooks had gone all out with a farewell meal of steak, corn on the cob and string beans. Mom and Dad were relieved that I was in good spirits and Dad remembered that I always did thrive on excitement and the unexpected. I reassured Mom, who was always eager for me to get ahead in the world, that I would still apply for regular O.C.S. or at least rise through the ranks in the infantry, the way Uncle Ernest did. We didn't talk about the additional hazards of being a replacement. We left it that college would have to wait.

When the train pulled into Camp Livingston two days later, I liked the feeling of all the pine trees everywhere. It was the end of January 1944, and pouring rain. Corporals and sergeants were everywhere, shouting orders to form up in four rows in front of each railroad car. A corporal and sergeant barked out our unit assignments and welcomed us to the 86th Infantry Division. I liked the shoulder insignia, a black hawk with wings spread on a red shield. Trucks took us into camp and to the squad huts of Easy company. The non-coms were older than us and not too happy being flooded with a deluge of 'college kids.' They strutted around in front of our formation shouting out the locations of latrines, mess hall, PX and the company office.

Then they did a rundown of the next day's schedule, laced with lots of sarcasm: "Now, we know you guys think you're hot shit with your big IQs and all, but we're gonna teach you 'common sense.' We're sorry as hell that you got bumped out of your nice cozy college dorms, but we'll try to make y'all comfortable."

"Some of your kind are already here, so now you can piss and moan together. The C.O., Captain Foxfield, wants to meet each of you tomorrow alphabetically, right after breakfast, so start lining up at the office by 0800 sharp. Any of you quiz kids got any questions?" No one opened their mouth. Then the final barb, "Well, wadda ya know, no questions. Oh, I'm sooo sorry. I forgot. You guys already know everything."

Later, in our squad hut we got better acquainted with other A.S.T.Pers and a couple of canceled student pilots. We all agreed that the initiation had begun and that our non-coms were pretty threatened by us, but we did have them outnumbered. We wrote letters home with our new address and went to sleep in familiar double-decker bunks with the equally familiar snoring.

Next morning, after breakfast, I was first in line alphabetically to meet our new C.O. Captain Foxfield was seated behind a desk with two other officers. Ushered in by the company clerk, I came to attention, saluted and said, "Private Robert Anderson, reporting as directed, sir."

The Captain then said, "At ease, private," and asked me to take a chair by his desk. Then, looking through what was obviously my service record he said, "Welcome to Company E, Private Anderson. How was your trip from Fort Benning?"

"Pretty good sir. It's good to be at least half-way home."

"Well, I guess this is going to be your home for now," he replied. I was beginning to think that this was the friendliest officer I had met so far. He smiled and nodded approvingly as he scanned my file. "Fort Benning is one hell of a school. I spent some time there in O.C.S.. I see here that you are qualified on every weapon that the infantry uses."

"Yes, Sir." Then he beamed broadly and looked at the other officers.

"Well gentlemen, we've got ourselves another expert marksman, and this one did it both left and right handed. Private Anderson!"

"Yes sir," I answered proudly.

And just as proudly, he said, " Congratulations! Tomorrow you start sniper training..."

BLACKHAWKS GO SOUTH

During the afternoon of my birthday, the Pershing tanks began to move out and army trucks began to arrive to take us to another combat area. Most of the northern German army that had been encircled in the 'pocket' were assembled in fields between Hagan and Altena, where they were being registered and moved to various P.O.W. camps. Their own mess trucks were cooking up food brought in by our supply trucks. I alternated between helping search prisoners, collecting weapons and operating our company radio. I also drew several shifts as Corporal of the Guard during the evening and night. Part of our responsibility was to keep SS troops separated from the Wehrmacht, and to keep prisoners from wandering off looking for friends. They seemed glad it was over. I was envious.

Lt. Houston leaked the word to us that we were to remain with the Eighteenth Airborne Corps and be taken by those trucks to board gliders for a landing behind German Lines, further to the East. Jerry asked sardonically if we would get suicide pay. From the moment we joined the Airborne Corps we were afraid this might happen. We also knew from survivors attached to our regiment that every glider landing was a crash landing, with many fatalities. In my crushing fatigue I had mumbled to Jerry, "Well, at least we know now how we're going to die." Moments of sleep were nightmares, all ending in grinding, fiery crashes.

I had also been awakened many times during the night to repair damaged weapons for several companies in my battalion. One armorer had been killed and another was missing-in-action. Most of the requests were for replacement parts that were lost during cleaning or damaged, such as shattered hand guards, broken firing pins and leather slings. The supply truck, my mobile workshop, carried boxes of spare parts as well as small oil cans and cotton cleaning patches for cleaning and oiling rifle bores. I was responsible for re-issuing M-1 rifles of dead G.I.'s to men whose weapons were beyond repair. Serial numbers were matched to specific owners, which provided another way to identify casualties if dog-tags were blown away or obliterated. This was my night job. I would be alternating radio operator shifts in the radio jeep on our trip.

A cold, rolling mist overhead had reflected the fires still burning in the nearby captured towns and illuminated the sky all night with an eerie orange glow. Our regiment held company formations in a large field on the outskirts of Hagan, just as sunrise added yellow to the color in the mist. Mail was distributed, as were blue and silver combat infantry badges which added ten dollars a month to our service pay. I was now getting seventy dollars a month. We were told that the Quartermaster clerk would set up a table to distribute pay to anyone wanting their money. This brought a burst of the first laughter I had heard in a long time. No line formed as the clerk sat nonchalantly reading a crumpled copy of the Stars and Stripes newspaper. Some of us did ask if we could see the latest Bill Mauldin cartoon of our infantry heroes, Willie and Joe.

Our company commander, Captain Sullivan, said he thought we would like some good news. He told us that in spite of what we had heard about a glider landing with the Eighteenth, the area of the landing had already been captured by an American division ahead of schedule. We would be heading South for further combat. Secrecy dictated that we know no more than this, in case we were captured. He cautioned that we would be on roads along the front lines all the way to our destination and might be pulled into combat anywhere, and to remain alert. Then came the welcome announcement that our mess truck had arrived and was serving breakfast. 'K' rations would have to do on our trip, so a line for hot food formed quickly.

While loading up on the trucks by squads, extra bandoleers of ammunition were being handed out by the supply crew. We were given back our gas masks, which had been picked up by a special detail after we threw them into ditches on our first day of fighting in the Rhur

Valley. A note was attached to each case warning us that we would be charged for any further "Abandonment of Government Property." This was our second laugh of the day. While waiting to move out on the fully packed trucks, I noticed a jeep moving slowly past us with Marty driving the Chaplain. He slowed down and I found out that he was now also the Chaplain's assistant because he could play the field organ. I asked about Colonel King. Shouting above the truck engines he said, "Remember when we dropped him off at the aid station, after we sewed his scalp back on? Well, he didn't get help. Just commandeered a jeep and went to Battalion Headquarters instead. When I saw him, he said we had done a hell of a job of sewing him up and the bleeding had stopped, but he had to get us out of this mess. Said he would get checked out later. He had one hell of a headache. I haven't seen him since the tanks came and got us. How's your wisdom tooth?"

I shouted back as he sped off, "It hurts— but it takes my mind off all this."

The close quarters on the truck helped us get warmer as we sat closely packed in two rows facing each other. The canvas top was rolled back so there could be many pairs of eyes looking out for trouble. As our convoy headed south from the smoking city of Hagan, we were moving between the familiar columns of refugees on both sides of the road, this time moving in opposite directions. There were the same stoic, haunted faces we had seen since crossing the Rhine. The processions included two-wheeled carts pulled by hand or animals, loaded wheelbarrows, and children's wagons loaded with huge bundles. Older men, women and children of all ages carried large packs and bundles. They moved slowly and quietly, seldom looking at us as we passed. Children scrambled for the chewing gum, candy and 'K' rations that we threw to them. I knew these people were the families of soldiers we had been fighting, but I could only see the faces of my parents, uncles, aunts, cousins, nieces and nephews. Many were injured and our medic jeeps often stopped to render emergency aid along the way.

After about an hour of travel we passed through a dense forest with deep trenches on each side of the road. Someone stood up, pointed to a trench and shouted, "Hey look!" There, in the trench were growing piles of gas masks thrown from the trucks ahead. Without a word all of the gas mask packs from our truck were flying through the air, with the warning messages still attached.

We watched as each truck following us erupted with the same shower of gas masks until a turn in the road blocked our view and interrupted our entertainment.

I decided to read my mail as many others were doing on the trip. As we all shared bits of information from home, I heard the usual mixture of good and bad news. I simply mentioned that my mother had baked a birthday cake for my birthday and had sent it a couple of weeks ago. I promised to share it if it ever arrived. Mom described the ranch in full bloom and Dad even added a page about the Hernandez family, who had written that they would be coming to help with the harvest again this year if they could save enough gasoline for the trip. He was sorry I had missed them last summer. Chita and Rose, my summertime girlfriends, were even prettier and helped take care of the horses. Dad hoped I would be home this summer. I dozed off thinking of the girls dancing around their campfire.

Our convoy of trucks, jeeps and armored personnel carriers stretched for many miles as we moved south and east toward Frankfurt. The double columns of refugees were thinner now and M.P.s were directing us at all major intersections. The sounds of artillery and mortars just a few miles away could be heard constantly above the growling whine of the trucks. Torrents of icy rain forced us to pull the canvas back over the top of the truck and sacrifice some of our view as we entered a very open length of road. The column slowed and we could hear explosions directly ahead. The Jerries were bombarding the convoy in front of us. The pre-targeted road allowed them to lob shells through the rain, probably directed by a lone observer hidden in the mountains above us.

As we crept closer to the target area, a rosy glow all around us in the now misty rain revealed five trucks and a jeep on fire, and pushed off of the road. Several had suffered direct hits. Dead and injured G.I.s were scattered everywhere. As we drove past I looked down into the remains of one truck and saw only the bottom parts of about ten bodies. A large shell had landed on the bed and exploded upward, tearing the bodies apart and scattering them over a large area. The water in the roadside ditch was blood red. Medics were loading the casualties into ambulances and a medical truck. Soon we were racing to catch up with the rest of the convoy. No one was speaking as we uncovered the top again, hoping to have time to jump out at the first sound of an incoming shell. Everyone agreed — this was the worst we had seen.

We slept on our trucks that night and I drew two radio watches, during which I received a lengthy message in five-letter code groups from Regimental Command. It turned out to be our marching orders for the next morning. It was April 20th and we had traveled two hundred miles. In roadside company formations at daybreak, we received our orders to leave the trucks and launch an attack toward Frankfurt. Our first objective was Wiesbaden and after that we were to capture a German prisoner compound of Allied prisoners of war on the other side of the city. Air support arrived in the form of B-24 and B-26 bombers. They unloaded their bombs on Wiesbaden and Frankfurt. Flare pistols in each Battalion signaled the attack and once again we were on the front line of combat.

Colorful scarves appeared almost simultaneously as we raced across the first field toward the city. As the bombers moved on P-38s and P-50s followed, coming in low over our heads and strafing the fields in front of us. Now we were on our own. The familiar "popping" of bullets going by dispelled any notion that this would be easy. Machine gun fire followed, along with saturation mortar fire. We were soon diving from one shell hole to another with quick spurts of sprinting in between. I watched as Tony's helmet was blown off of his head by a bullet that carved a crease along the top. "Damn, that was close!" he said as he crawled over to where it had landed and admired the shiny groove. "If that didn't get me, nothing will," he shouted as he got up and ran all the way to the first building at the entrance to the city. Before we got to him he had knocked out a machine gun crew and a mortar nest. His lapse of caution had just assured him of a Bronze Star, and may have saved our lives.

We were part of the first assault wave and fighting house to house. I somehow felt less vulnerable here than sitting in that truck convoy. We all carried an extra supply of hand grenades so we always lobbed a grenade through a door or window before we entered. At one house, where we had seen several German soldiers run in, I climbed a convenient ladder next to the chimney and dropped two grenades down into the fireplace. Soldiers and soot exploded out the front door. All were wounded and surrendered. Once again our bright scarves seemed to create confusion in the disciplined Germans and gave us an advantage. We also screamed a lot and laughed like maniacs as we shot at anything that moved. Even as we advanced, there were times when withering fire would force us to dive into craters or doorways and to stay put. As usual I kept an eye on the location of corporal Brewster who still glowered at me whenever we were near each other. I remembered his promise to "get me." He knew I was watching him. He was now racing up this street ahead of me. I aimed my rifle at him as he paused at one corner waiting for machine gun fire to ease up and seriously considered shooting him to eliminate the threat he posed for me. No one would know. Everyone was too busy dodging bullets. Instead I noticed a sniper aiming at him from a high window ledge and I shot him instead. Then I moved my squad up the street bewildered by my action. Why hadn't I let the sniper end my constant worry?

Then there was a house with a large white flag hanging out of the window. Instead of kicking in the door, I knocked loudly and the door was opened quickly by a young woman whose flashing blue eyes showed both fear and defiance. Just behind her stood an older couple, probably her grandparents. I asked in German if they had any German soldiers in the building. They shook their heads. Part of my squad followed me into a large entry room and searched the rest of the house. I motioned with my rifle for the young woman to preceed me down some stairs into the cellar. That is where we often found soldiers hiding. I wanted to use her as a shield. She began to protest which set off wailing and pleading from the couple. My squad rallied as we now became more suspicious and they leveled their rifles and told the couple to shut up. The crying and pleas continued. The woman walked hesitantly down the stairs as I watched carefully for whomever they were hiding. A careful search revealed no soldiers. As I lowered my rifle in relief and started to go back up the stairs she started to cry and thanked me. I raised my shoulders with my open hands up questioning, "Why?" With a relieved smile she demonstrated with graphic sign language that she and her grandparents thought we were going to rape her in the basement. Back upstairs, when all was cleared up there were smiles all around and the now familiar, "We hate Hitler, we hate the war."

Out in the street again we noticed that the shooting had subsided. White flags were appearing rapidly as we walked up the street. A messenger told us that the Germans were retreating and that we could just walk through the town. House-to-house searching would be picked up by the second assault wave. We had time to gaze at the destruction by our Air Force bombs and the ghostly shapes of bombed-out buildings The citizens were evacuating dead bodies from many of the buildings and neighborhood emergency crews had set up medical aid stations where people were lined up waiting for treatment. We passed a couple of German tanks still smoldering, with crew members dead on the ground or hanging out of the turrets. Our bombers had been very thorough.

The faint sound of organ music drifted up the street toward us from somewhere up ahead. It grew louder as my company approached a large and ancient church standing defiantly in the midst of complete destruction. Smoke, dust and ashes mixed with occasional rain drops added to the desolation. Jerry and I decided to veer off and investigate the source of the music. Climbing over rubble and still watchful for snipers we pushed aside some timbers blocking the front door and entered the church. The ceiling was now on the floor. We walked over the debris to the altar area and found Marty playing a large organ. Then I saw that he had an audience. Colonel King was sitting in the front pew, his red scarf wrapped around his head like a turban. He motioned us to join him, saying he wanted to hear the rest of his favorite Bach Fugue. Marty was panting from pumping the foot bellows so I sat down to help.

With the increased airflow, he increased the volume and added many bass stops. The now thunderous music reverberated around the standing walls and loosened a remaining piece of the roof which crashed down to the floor near the front entrance. Marty didn't seem to notice and Colonel King, with a broad grin said, "Well, he brought down the God-damn house with that one!" When Marty finished he joined us as we learned that our Colonel had finally seen a real doctor, who told him he was healing nicely but that he had never seen olive-drab sewing-thread sutures before. He thanked us again for saving his scalp. As he sped off with his driver I asked Marty if he would play the organ for my wedding after the war. He said he would be "delighted." He also said he had lost track of the chaplain and his jeep and asked if he could join us for awhile.

Everyone was pleased to have Marty join us on the truck. We had all seen him in action and many of us had already been patched up by him. He was fairly tall, and pudgy, but as we had seen, he was amazingly agile on the battlefield. It was a good time to find out more about him. I learned that he had become a medic because he was a conscientious objector. He had been scheduled for pre-med at U.C.L.A. when A.S.T.P. collapsed. His family owned a paper mill in San Francisco and he had no brothers or sisters. He also wanted to be a concert pianist and had already been a professional organist. Marty liked it that I had also played professionally even though he couldn't understand why anybody would want to play drums.

It was near evening as we approached the location of the Allied P.O.W. camp. We were the first to reach the sinister-looking, fenced-in compound, surrounding at least fifty wood and lath prisoner cabins. The Germans were in the process of leaving as we arrived, so there was some exchange of small arms fire as the prisoners inside were loudly cheering. An armored troop carrier moved up to the front gate where a crewman threw a large grappling hook onto the main gate and backed up, ripping down the gate and some of the fencing. Over a thousand American, English, Canadian and Polish fliers came streaming out of the gate cheering and taunting us for taking so long to free them. We shouted back that we were sorry to take so long but we had gone to a concert in Wiesbaden. The fliers ran past us, ignoring the tables being set up to register them. They were headed for the city of Wiesbaden and any bars and restaurants that might be open. I helped Marty find the Chaplain who was standing in the stream of released fliers, offering his services.

We took over buildings in Weisbaden for the night. Many of the freed fliers were roaming the city streets and had obviously found plenty of liquor stored away. I found a very soft bed in a room near the living-room fireplace and claimed it for a good night of sleep. Around the fireplace were my buddies from radio, telephone, and I and R squads. Brewster was out drinking. As I was sitting off to one side and reading my mail again, Chester came over and sat down near me. I realized I hadn't given him any mail for a few days so I handed him the latest from my Mom and Dad. While I was writing, Chester was reading the one with the page from Dad. I told him how happy I was when Dad wrote because he wasn't very sure of his spelling. I mentioned that both my Mom and Dad only went to school through the sixth grade. After re-reading the letter several times, Chester said, "Andy, your Dad mentioned that there Hernandez family, ya know,—they come fer the harvest and ya know,—them girls,—Chita and Rose? Could ya tell me about that?—like them stories ya tell Jerry and J.C. 'bout the ranch sometimes?"

I shrugged off my drowsiness, threw some wood on the fire and said, "Chester, I would love to tell you about the best summer I ever had with Chita and Rose."

So I did.

CHITA AND ROSE

Summer vacation was my salvation. A brand new word had been used during the school year by my teacher, Mrs. Bronte. "Hyperactive." It had taken more than a dozen parent-teacher conferences with my mother to keep me enrolled in my country school for the year. "Restlessness, talking all the time, poor concentration, dropping things and procrastination," were a few of the specific charges. Spending the year with my desk in the cloakroom and being grounded for all recesses and lunch hours hadn't helped much. Mom, with her sweetness and sincere concern, always managed to buy me more time. Once she even got Mrs. Bronte to erase one of the zeros from the number of minutes of grounding I had accumulated. Mom seldom mentioned anything about her meetings. I think she liked it when I broke the rules. Now it was all over for the next three months.

I always knew when freedom was on the way. It started with my birthday in the middle of April when our lilac bushes bloomed. I had turned twelve. Then the peach, plum, apricot and pear trees bloomed. The grape vines were leafing out so fast that you could almost see them growing. The horses and mules were shedding their winter coats and I could run around the ranch barefooted. My final report card had even shown good grades, in spite of the comments by Mrs. Bronte. The King's River and the canal near our house were both running full, ready and waiting for swimming and fishing. Dad was singing all the time, happy at the prospect of a bumper crop.

It was the first day of vacation and I didn't have to get up early. The sun was already about two feet above the Sierra mountain range and starting to warm up the San Joaquin Valley. I had never learned how to loll in bed and my legs were already twitching to get started. Then it hit me. Not only was this the very beginning of the summer, but Jesus

Hernandez and his family would be arriving today from Chandler, Arizona, to help us with our harvest. Except for last year, they had been coming every year, for as long as I could remember. Jesus and his wife, Maria, had two sons and two daughters, all married, and about fifteen grandchildren. Every year the family was larger. Sometimes they brought other relatives. I loved the excitement they brought with them. And I loved Chita and Rose. They would be about thirteen and fourteen now. When I saw them two years ago, Chita, as brown as the rest, had blond hair and blue eyes and bragged about being a family embarrassment. Rose had large brown eyes and hair to match, and dimples. They were both good-looking and were always laughing and singing. Summer was not nearly as much fun last year without them. They had written that their truck and pickups couldn't make the trip. Their brothers, sisters and cousins were fun too, but I liked them the best. They loved to tease me and make me blush.

My dog Rusty arrived just then, jumped on my bed with a growl and pulled the covers off of me. I guess Dad had decided it was time for me to be up. I wrestled with Rusty for awhile and then put on my levis and white T-shirt, my uniform for the summer. I didn't bother with shoes since I already had thick calluses from going barefooted. Pretty soon, even puncture vines wouldn't bother me. When I joined the family for breakfast it was obvious that everyone was excited about the arrival of the Hernandez family. Herb was looking forward to seeing Juan who was just about his age and hoped he still played the flute. Dad hoped to talk Jesus into finding a place to live near us for the winter instead of returning to Chandler. He had talked to other ranchers who could give them work during the winter. They could help us with our round-ups, pruning and hay hauling. Dad liked to help people. Mom wanted to hire the oldest sister, Carmen, to help her with housework and all the cooking for the hired hands this summer. I didn't have to say what I wanted. Everyone knew I would be all but living with the Hernandezs' and working in the fields with the kids. I did say I couldn't wait to taste their tortillas and beans.

"Yeah, Bud," Herb teased, "But I'll bet you mostly can't wait to see Chita and Rose."

"Maybe," I agreed, trying to act like it was no big deal. My face got hot anyway and I hated him until he pretended not to notice.

It was mid-afternoon when the caravan came chugging and steaming into our yard. Two dilapidated Chevy trucks, two pickups and a multicolored sedan ground to a stop. Tired and dusty passengers of all ages shouted "Hola," as Jesus and Maria slowly stepped out of the newest truck and shook hands with Mom and Dad and Herb. I had always joined in the greeting in the past but for some reason this year I felt shy, especially when I saw how much Chita and Rose had changed. I just watched everything from the shadows inside the open barn door.

After the noisy greeting and a handshake, the harvesting agreement was quickly decided. Then, with Jesus and Maria back in the truck and with my Dad on the runningboard, the steaming procession moved down a hill to the nearest corner of the orchard. Everyone had a job as they pitched five tents made of large colorful patches of red, yellow, orange and green canvas and cloth. As usual the tents were arranged in a large circle. A concrete ring, about three feet in diameter and a foot deep, that had been parked at the corner of the orchard since their last visit was rolled to the center of the circle. When laid flat it became a fire pit for bonfires and cooking. I managed to milk our two cows and help Herb feed the horses and mules in the barn without being seen by our new arrivals. I decided to wait until it was darker before saying hello.

While we were eating supper everyone came racing out of the tents and through the yard as they headed for a swim in the canal along the front of our ranch. Now, I was sorry that I had gone into hiding and missed out on the fun. From our kitchen window we could see Jesus, Maria and a couple of their older relatives lighting a bonfire in the fire ring. They were using the peach wood Dad had saved for them during the winter. I decided to go down to the outdoor haystack near the camp before everyone else returned from the swim. Dusk was deepening as I found the cave I had made in the stack of baled hay, a few feet above ground and about fifty feet away from the entrance to the camp. I thought I might just watch the entertainment safely from my hideout, and then just drift into camp later without being so obvious. A large cast-iron bean pot, suspended with bailing-wire from a peach-limb tripod, was already boiling. An iron griddle, placed across one side of the fire-ring, was already filled with handmade tortillas. My stomach began to growl as the waves of cooking smells reached my perch.

The swimmers, refreshed by the cold water runoff from the nearby Sierras, raced back into camp and went to work on the tortillas and beans. Just then I saw Dad walk into camp with a large tray of fresh beef slices and a box of vegetables from our garden. With whoops of delight, the meat was cut into cubes and added to the bean pot. String beans, carrots and potatoes were added next. When Dad left, he was carrying a bowl of chili beans, the second part of a swap that would happen almost daily for the rest of the summer. What the hell was I doing, watching all of this when I could have been in the middle of it. Something was happening to me. I liked being five inches taller than two years ago, but I hated this shyness.

I was about to force myself out of my cave when all the young people disappeared into the tents. When they came out they were in bright-colored clean clothes and some were carrying guitars and fiddles. Juan had his flute. They joined the older musicians and began to play as more wood was added to the fire. I knew what was coming. The 'ground packing' ritual was about to begin. At first it was just like two years ago. Everyone started moving around the fire, stomping their feet to pack down the soft plowed earth in front of the tents. After several trips around the fire-ring, the 'stompers' had packed the ground into a much smoother surface. Then something different happened. The older people sat down and the younger ones began more rhythmic steps, moving in time with the music. They were dancing, and they also kept looking at one particular tent expectantly as they glided around the fire.

Carmen, Pilar, Chita and Rose exploded from the tent in long, flowing, brightly colored dresses. They twirled, dipped and skipped around the fire as they mingled with the younger kids. A shower of live sparks streamed up into the darkening night as Jesus and Juan added fresh wood to the fire. Everyone was singing and clapping now to the strong, steady beat of the dancers. Some of the older boys joined the dancing and moved against the circle, giving each girl a twirl as they passed. Sequins sewn on the flaring skirts reflected the fire, scattering light all over the orchard like fireflies. The girls, with long un-braided hair flying, were holding up their skirts and swishing them from left to right, teasing the guys. The slightly damp soil was soon packed into a smooth, clay-like surface. The dancing, singing and strumming of guitars grew louder and faster. I couldn't take my eyes off of Chita and Rose. They couldn't be the same girls I had splashed around with in muddy irrigation ditches two years before. The long, tanned legs and arms, moving so gracefully were new. And so were their breasts and red lipstick. I knew some of the songs and couldn't help singing along with them. Too loud I guess, because in the middle of La Cuchauracha I was discovered.

Chita and Rose had spotted me and with squeals of delight came running over to the haystack and dragged me out of my cave. They hugged me and teased me for hiding—insisting that I join the party. The family chorused a lively greeting as the girls led me into the circle with their arms still around me. Fortunately, the orange glow of the fire hid my blushing. These were, after all, the first hugs from girls who were not my cousins. As they smacked loud kisses on my burning cheeks I wished I could get rid of the stupid grin on my face. Jesus gave me a sympathetic smile and said, "Don't worry, Bobby, they're just having fun." They both had more of everything than I remembered. Their eyes were even more mischievous and sparkling. Their laughing voices, more musical and flirtatious than ever. The sweet smell of new sweat mingled with the scent of roses in their hair as they brushed their new breasts against my arms. I felt kind of dizzy, with giant butterflies in my stomach and a weird itch in my throat. I tingled all over and thought I was going to explode. *Maybe I'm getting sick,* I thought.

Just then, Chita, whose blond hair was more red now said, "Bobby, you look kind'a pale. I think you need some food." She grabbed a bowl and spooned out the chili stew. As the music became quieter I managed to get out my first complete sentence.

"It was sure quiet here last summer and you've sure changed a lot," I said, looking at the girls.

"Whadda you mean, 'we've' changed." Rose was now seated on one side of me. "How about you? You're a foot taller than last time."

"Kinda skinny though," Chita chimed in.

"But we'll fatten you up this summer. Got a girlfriend, Bobby? Come on, you can tell us. Is she as pretty as us?" Rose giggled.

When I said I didn't have one, Chita acted shocked, stood up, did two spins and landed on my lap saying, "Oh yes you do. You've got us—and for the whole summer." I imagined that my grin now was even sappier and I didn't have the slightest idea of what to do. Everyone was watching and waiting for my response.

I shook my head, summoned up my courage and announced boldly for the family, "I guess I could do worse." Then I tickled her in the ribs. From the whoops and applause, I gathered that I had passed the test.

Intervening finally, Jesus said, "Bobby, we'll expect you for dinner every night. But you'll have to bring some drums."

The peach harvest began the very next morning. I was up early every morning, rushing through breakfast to get to work in the orchards so I could casually intercept Chita and Rose who always seemed to know exactly what I was doing. I was usually greeted with, "Hola! Bobby. Did you miss me?" and, "Would you come up on the ladder and help me." That was with other people around. When I was alone with one or the other they would grab my hand matter-of-factly or put an arm on my shoulder, which somehow seemed to quiet the butterflies. Dad was impressed with how many chores and field jobs I volunteered for. He said he had never seen me work so hard. He also asked me if I had noticed how pretty Chita and Rose had become. I was about to shrug off his comment as no big deal, but the twinkle in his eye told me not to bother. He knew the truth, and besides, he didn't tease me about girls. It was better to "come clean" with my Dad.

Usually by mid-morning we had picked enough peaches for a day's cutting. The filled boxes were hauled on a horse-drawn wagon to the cutting shed. There they were placed on racks on each side of wooden drying trays. We older kids were the cutters. Each of us stood at a box, spinning a peach with one hand around a knife in the other hand. Then we flipped out the pit and laid the two halves on the tray, all in one motion. The men, including Herb and Juan, lifted boxes on and off racks, and stacked filled trays on a small railroad cart. They also yelled at us for throwing peach pits at each other. At the end of the day, it took many of us to push the cart loaded with fifty trays along the rails and into the smoke house where burning sulfur began the drying process. "Why sulfur?" Rose asked, wrinkling her nose. "It smells so terrible. I'm never going to eat dried peaches again."

Trying not to sound too important, I explained, "Well, all I know is that burning sulfur kills bacteria in fresh peaches, so they won't rot when we put the trays in the sun tomorrow. You can't taste the sulfur. They just dry up like beef-jerky."

"Oh, Bobby," Chita said mockingly, as she batted her eye lashes. "You're soooo smart." I threw a peach at her as she went into hysterics. We exchanged winter stories, and when they heard of my feud with Mrs. Bronte and my year long isolation in the cloak room they were outraged. They wanted to find out where she lived and tomato her house. When I was around them, I didn't notice the hundred-and-ten degree temperature or the itchy peach fuzz floating around the shed.

As summer led into the grape harvest, much of our time was spent under Thompson seedless vines, picking grapes to spread on wooden trays for drying into raisins. There were many opportunities to be with them alone. It was easy to duck under a vine and work toward either Chita or Rose. Once I carried two bottles of homemade root beer in my lug box and pulled them out when I met up with Rose. She was delighted. She leaned across my box, threw both arms around me, gave me a kiss on the mouth and began drinking her root beer, all in one motion. I don't remember ever feeling so good. She saw me looking at the open buttons on her shirt and asked if I would like to see what had happened since two years ago. While I was struggling with my embarrassment, she opened her shirt and asked me what I thought. I managed to say, "They're nice. Do they get in the way?"

She looked down at them and replied, "A little. You wanna touch 'em?"

"No, that's O.K," I heard myself saying, even as my hand began to move.

She said, "Oh," with a tone of surprise then smiled, shrugged her shoulders and buttoned up her shirt. Feeling very disappointed, I thought that maybe Mrs. Bronte was right. I did speak before thinking.

We finished our root beer and each started a new row. I could hear her singing in Spanish as she worked, gleefully substituting "Bobby" for "Carlos" in her song. I promised myself I would learn more Spanish as I moved along under the vines, calling myself chicken and regretting my missed opportunity. In my dreams that night, I wasn't so chicken. The next day Chita arranged to work in my row and we soon met. She teased me about Rose and the kiss. Then she said, "What about me?" I received my second kiss under the vines but no extra offers.

On the Fourth of July the girls, as messengers for the family, came banging on our kitchen door to invite us for a campfire dinner and fireworks. We accepted the invitation providing they would come up to our place afterwards for dessert. Since nobody was working on the 4th they asked if I would teach them to ride Blue Rhone, our most gentle horse. They learned quickly in their noisy fashion, with lots hugs and pats for Blue who followed them all the way to their tent, where they put on bathing suits for a dip in the canal. Everybody, including my folks, suited up and went swimming. I stayed mostly in the water so the girls wouldn't notice my skinniness. They were delighted when Rose managed to pull my bathing suit half-way off. I made a token grab at the top of her suit but the whole thing came off. She ducked under the water sputtering and faked being indignant saying, "No fair, Bobby. You had your chance!"

That night, after an afternoon of siestas and the arrival of cooling evening breezes, a full moon rose over the Sierras adding even more excitement to the campfire dinner. Watermelon and peach ice-cream dessert followed, under the Chinese lanterns in our yard.

At midnight, with everyone asleep, I was awakened by the girls, scratching at the screened window of my upstairs bedroom. When they said they wanted to go horseback riding it took me a minute to realize they weren't actually in my dream. I rushed to dress, crawled out my window, and followed them over the roof of the kitchen and down the walnut tree. They insisted we all ride Blue down to the river. With Rose in front of me and Chita behind me we headed for the dark outline of cottonwood trees along the Kings River. As I prepared to take Blue into the water, the girls told me to wait. They slid off and without hesitation peeled off all their clothes and asked me to hoist them back on, front and back as before. Chita, lifted my T-shirt and I let her pull it over my head but they left me with my levis. I wondered if they could hear my heart pounding as I tried to be nonchalant.

Blue knew the way to my bamboo island in the middle of the river. As she swam, we floated off of her back, holding on to tufts of mane. The girls were fearless in the dark water and completely comfortable with their nakedness. When we could feel the sloping beach we walked onto the island with Blue. He led us through the pathway into a clearing in the center of the grove. We sat on a raft I had made of bamboo bundles and hidden in the clearing. When I told them I had floated on it several miles downstream they made me promise I would do that with them in the daytime. We left Blue munching on bamboo sprouts while we sat on the small, sandy beach. The moonlight glistened on the girls' bodies and I tried not to stare. They were so natural and so pretty as they chattered about their life in Chandler. They sat close to me and in some strange way that calmed me down a little. With their clothes on they were teasing and flirtatious. Without clothes they were more normal. Their happiness helped me fight off feelings that we were doing something wrong. I asked if we could keep this a secret. They agreed as Chita said, "Yeah, our folks would probably think we were 'doin it.'"

On the return trip Blue pulled us along as before and the water seemed much warmer. We even let go of his mane and swam beside him. Chita saw a log floating downstream, screamed and grabbed onto me until I convinced her it was harmless. Then she kept one hand on my shoulder until we reached the shore. I liked that a lot.

Back on Blue with our clothes on again, we rode as one while the girls took turns explaining to me about going to 'first,' 'second,' 'third' and 'all the way.' "Did you ever go all the way?" I asked.

Truly shocked, they both protested, "Oh, no, Bobby! How could you think that? We're both virgins!"

Then Chita squeezed me from behind and teased, "Besides, we're waiting for you to grow up." I told them we would have to walk Blue until he dried off or my Dad would figure out what happened, so we took many detours and got back to the corral about 3:00 a.m. As I quietly crawled into my bed I wondered if other guys had ever loved two girls together. This was the best day of my life.

HIT AND RUN WITH PATTON

We could see smoke rising from the city of Frankfurt as we approached from Weisbaden. After bidding farewell to the P.O.W. camp we had liberated, we were picked up by a convoy of fast-moving trucks heading south and west. When our artillery bombardment of Frankfurt was halted, a division from our right flank had moved in and taken the city. We circled around and kept moving east toward Wurzburg. Colonel King brought the word to each company that we were now attached to Patton's Third Army and were entering the southern part of Germany called Bavaria. Even through the rain and dense fog I could see many unusual features in the countryside. Forests were dense and dark. Fields were deep green and manicured right up to the roads. Large sculpted hills supported small castles and more forests. Villages and hamlets along the road were all surrounded by medieval walls covered with ivy. Our rumbling, armed presence seemed like a profane intrusion.

We rolled through ten villages and hamlets before reaching Wurzburg, all in one day, April 21st. Most of them contained rear-guard troops, often SS that offered brief, but fierce resistance. At each village our plan of attack was the same. We would jump off of the trucks and spread out in two single lines about six feet apart. While standing in that endless firing line and waiting for the "Move Out" order I noticed all of the different colored scarves on the men in my company. Something was very familiar about what was happening. Something before the war.

Before I could remember, the order was given to attack with Marching Fire, an infantry term for shooting from the hip while running. The first line would take off running toward the main entrance to the town firing all eight rounds in a clip continuously before diving for cover. Then the second wave would attack moving through and beyond

117

the first wave before hitting the ground. We would reload from our ammo belts or bandoleers while on the ground. The result was almost continuous rifle and sub-machine gun fire at the defenders. This kind of attack always felt suicidal, charging directly into enemy fire but we actually had fewer casualties this way. Another advantage was not having to keep an eye on Brewster as much. I worried more about him when we were house-to-house where he could pick me off when no one would see him.

We found most German troops outside the houses and shot them instantly if they didn't drop their guns and raise their arms. Many were lying around, wounded by our attacking barrage. In one town a wounded German soldier with SS markings on his collar raised up as he pulled the pin on a potato-masher grenade and tossed it at us. I shot him in the forehead as Jerry scooped up the grenade and threw it over a wall into a yard where it exploded. Screams that followed could have been those of a hiding Kraut or a civilian. We didn't check to see. I chose to believe that civilians would be in their cellars. As we reached the other end of a town, our trucks would move through the main street and pick us up again and move us quickly to the next village.

The ride provided a chance to rest and also to stock up on ammunition. 'K' rations were passed around during these rides and often refused. However, when it became clear that we were not going to see our mess trucks, we would rip open the waxed cardboard containers with their contents of canned beef or canned eggs and ham, hard crackers and not so fresh candy. The little package of four Lucky Strike or Old Gold cigarettes could be bartered off to the smokers or handed out to the refugees. In spite of Eisenhower's promise of one hot meal a day for combat troops, we had not had a hot meal for almost two weeks. As fast-moving front line troops we knew we were not easily accessible and had learned to forage for food where we could find it. Many farms were relieved of chickens, eggs and black pumpernickel bread. Word of our technique for French fried potatoes had spread quickly throughout the division.

As our trucks reached the outskirts of Wurzburg, we pulled into a forest for the night. The trucks were running out of gas and the tankers didn't show up. Also food was running low. We were clearly outrunning our supply lines. Sitting around low, hidden fires everyone was doing what we always did when we had a break; dismantling our rifles and cleaning them. Then the larger weapons were cleaned, the bazookas, Browning automatic rifles, sixty millimeter mortars and our flame thrower. We all lived in fear that they would jam in the middle of a fire fight and no one enjoyed the prospect of a bayonet duel.

With our victory in the Rhur behind us we were once again carrying many German weapons. Especially the rapid firing 'burp' guns. They would fire twice as fast as our M-3s and Thompsons. Four-man patrols were sent out to check on any covert action by the Germans, but also to hunt for the small Bavarian deer in the forest. The success of our patrol was evident in the venison being roasted over the fires like marshmallows on long sticks. Our truck drivers, mostly black, were all expert mechanics and used every break to replace parts and tune their engines. During the night, another division on our left flank swept into Wurzburg after an Allied bombing raid and captured the town. A gasoline tanker driver who had driven nonstop for twenty-four hours had arrived and filled the truck tanks. We loaded up before daybreak, munching on cold venison with new orders to Nuremberg.

We headed south toward Ansbach, just behind the front line all the way on treacherous, muddy roads filled with artillery and bomb craters. We passed a number of trucks that were disabled and one that had slid off the road and turned over, killing some of the guys and pinning others in the mud where they were screaming for help. Two other trucks with winches were trying to pull it off of them. About twenty GIs were using tree limbs struggling to lift the truck. I hated riding in those trucks. There was no place to hide. We were on those trucks for eight hours, covering thirty-five miles. About two hours out of Ansbach, a single German fighter plane came in low over the rear of our convoy and strafed the entire convoy. We were not hit but we heard a couple of truck engines ahead of us explode. There was a huge explosion as the pilot scored a hit on one of our ammunition trucks. Debris rained down on us with clinking sounds on our helmets. We soon passed the trucks that had been hit and many other trucks that were attending to men wounded by the strafing. The ammunition truck destroyed the elevated road when it blew up and a precarious detour around the spot was created in the muddy field.

As this point my turn at radio watch came up and I found the radio jeep to feel much less vulnerable than the truck. It was also relieving to talk with other operators. These were times when I could have a clearer sense of what was going on than when on rifle duty. I learned that at Ansbach, just a few miles ahead, we would be relieved for a day or two to rest and receive replacements and mail from home. A hot meal was also promised. Outside Ansbach, with assurance of a full night's sleep, we pitched pup-tents for the first time at the front. With each of us carrying one-half of a tent, called a shelter-half, one tent pole and three wooden pins we teamed up with a partner, buttoned the two halves together and erected a two man tent. It felt strange to be out of the rain, and even warm.

Mail was distributed in the chow line as we lined up for hot roast beef, sweet potatoes, green beans and home made biscuits. Chester would simply walk up and down the line handing out the mail with his good-natured comments on what each letter probably contained. When he came to my packet of letters he said, "Andy! Hugs and kisses from freckle-eyes in Dinuba, California." Then he paused over a letter studying it in amazement. Shooting a glance at me he announced. "Corporal Chester, a s'prise from California." Everyone cheered because Chester had never received any mail himself. Later he showed me the letter. It had been written by my mom after I told her about Chester. She had written about life on the ranch as if he was a part of the family. He was soon busy writing Mom an answer. Whenever we received mail from home we would all separate and find a quiet, private place to reconnect with our families.

Hearing from our loved ones was a mixed blessing. It was good to feel close to our families and to re-enter that other world, even briefly. However, it also dissolved our numbness and allowed the reality of this world to be felt again. News from home often carried a wallop for my buddies. Gary's father was killed in a car accident. Gil had become the father of a baby girl. Victor's brother was killed in a landing in the

South Pacific. Ron received a 'Dear John' letter from his fiancee. She was planning to marry someone else. Foster was very excited with news from his girlfriend that she was three months pregnant, until he realized he hadn't seen her for five months. If we weren't coping with our own news we were helping our buddies with theirs. Chaplain Sanders was always circling around when mail was delivered, ready with understanding and sometimes practical help in getting guys sent home for 'hardship' reasons. I always felt more fearful and self-protective after reading mail from home. Once I carried letters for three days before reading them. Not on this day however. My protection had dissolved while reading Mom's letter to Chester so I read my mail.

My folks had heard that our 86th Division was part of Patton's Third Army. Drew Pearson had announced that we had been on the German autobahn headed for Berlin and that Eisenhower had stopped our race to beat the Russians and sent us into southern Germany to attack the SS stronghold there. That was more than we had been told. Mom told me that Ray Morton, a classmate, had been killed in the South Pacific. Dad added a note about the success of the new kind of paper they were using to wrap around new grape vines to keep rabbits from eating them. Herb wrote of his worry about my being in combat and didn't want me to volunteer for anything. He was still upset about being stuck on Guam.

To Mom and Dad I wrote, "Well, I lost a few friends today but it feels like the worst is over. We are with Patton and moving fast. Sorry to hear about the Kingsburg guys but glad to hear about the new paper for the grape vines. You know, folks, today when we were approaching a town with our whole battalion spread out in one line of attack I remembered the old rabbit drives. I'm glad you came up with that oil-paper idea Dad, so we could stop killing rabbits. You really helped engineer a whole new idea. Well, we had a chance to rest up and eat some hot meals for a change. Plan to take a helmet bath tomorrow. Chester was really excited about the letter from you, Mom. Thanks for doing that. He really has no family at all. Glad you have spent some time with Margie and her folks. I really miss her too. Love to the best parents anybody ever had. Don't worry about me. I'll keep my head down. Love, Bob."

The next day, many of us took "helmet baths," the first in weeks. The water from the nearby river was icy-cold but served the purpose. There were meetings to inform us of our next battle plan and to update us on the war in general. Someone read a clipping from the New York Times about the 86th division having been on the road to Berlin and then diverted into Bavaria. Our new objective was to drive through the Germans all the way into Austria. We would leave the next day for Nuremberg for mop up and then south toward Munich. We had several rivers to cross and had a review session of our ranger training with river assault boats. It wasn't expected that any bridges would be left. Engineers would now be with us all the time.

Another convoy of trucks arrived with supplies and replacements for the men we had lost. I felt curiously disinterested in their arrival. They were a startling reminder of the friends we had lost. They were clean, their clothes were clean, and they seemed altogether too young to be here. They looked at us in awe and were eager to be accepted. They were even carrying their gas mask cases. As the company clerk, Chester was signing them in and directing them to their respective squads. "Glad to have you in my outfit," he told them cheerfully. He seemed to live in another world where he loved everybody. He had the same friendly greeting for German prisoners. He was especially protective of new replacements and in comparison, I became aware of my callousness in not wanting to know their names or even talk to them, knowing they would soon be dead. All I could see when I looked at them were dead, rumpled and bloody figures lying in a field with their helmets on their rifles.

These "kids" had only six weeks of training, no combat experience and were very scared. Then I remembered how it felt to be invisible with the vets in the hospital at Le Havre. Pushing through my reticence I decided to get acquainted with the ones assigned to my squad, Rick, a radio operator and Carlos, a machine-gunner. I also thought it made sense to pass on combat tricks that weren't in the training manuals, such as: "Don't bunch up and make an easy target; Wrap tape around your hand grenades so a pin won't come out accidentally; Leave your chin straps unfastened at all times so a concussion won't catch your helmet and break your neck, or so an infiltrator can't grab the front of your helmet from behind and break your neck by snapping it back; Don't ever salute officers in combat—that's like pointing out an officer to a sniper; and don't stop to help the wounded, the medics will be along and you must keep fighting." As better fighters, maybe they would save us sometime rather than put us in danger.

We also introduced our replacements to the joys of loading machine-gun belts. Everyone took turns on the belt loader whenever we camped. A tripod contraption, mounted with a loading mechanism mounted on top, had a metal seat for the operator to sit on while grinding away with two rotary handles. Thirty caliber shells would be poured into a feeder box on top as the empty belt was drawn through the machine. The shells would be shoved into the moving canvas belt as quickly as the operator could turn the handles. It was such hard work that we all lined up to take turns. We never wanted to run out of machine gun belts.

The following day, after a full night's sleep and a hot breakfast of fresh scrambled eggs, bacon and leftover biscuits we were on the road to Nuremberg. This time we were on a main road that by-passed smaller villages and within a couple of hours we were in the center of the city circling inside the huge, historical stadium with the tall towers and platform where Hitler had given many speeches. We spread out to secure all of the buildings in this sector and to eliminate any rear-guard groups and snipers. All we found were dead Germans and GIs from the battle yesterday. In a Gestapo headquarters building we found bodies of SS troopers, and a table full of important maps showing the location of our units and also theirs. Chester volunteered to run these to Battalion headquarters. With my rifle butt I broke the glass out of a coffee table and ripped out the black and white swastika flag underneath. I stuffed this in my field jacket as we headed back to our trucks, but noticed that a couple of the towers still had long ceremonial red and black swastika flags on them. I ran over and pulled down one of them for a souvenir. It was then that I noticed that Colonel King had set up headquarters in his jeep in the very center of the stadium. He was meeting with all company commanders. The bright red turban was still on his head.

Our orders were to move due south immediately with our same "hit and run" offensive. The first three towns offered light resistance and seemed unprepared for our arrival. We found larger numbers of German troops but they gave up quickly in the face of our running and shooting attack. We were now slowed a bit with many prisoners to process but we still moved on. Rick and Carlos no longer looked new. They were covered with mud and blood like the rest of us but were still alive. Colonel King and his jeep entered our convoy four trucks ahead of us and led us off the road and into the fourth town after ordering the trucks ahead to proceed to the next village.

Without stopping to let us out for our attack, he led us straight into the walled city at high speed with all of our trucks looking like large porcupines with the rifles sticking out in all directions. It soon became clear that the town was still occupied by Germans, along with trucks, armored carriers and a couple of tanks as we came roaring through. They were caught off guard and so were we. For a moment we just stared at each other. Everyone thinking the same thing, "Do I surrender or demand yours?" Then we quickly aimed our rifles and sub-machine guns at them as we heard Colonel King making the decision for all of us by bellowing orders to surrender. Weapons were dropped and arms moved slowly up into the air, almost in unison. With their breakfasts still cooking over open fires, over a thousand prisoners were rounded up and sent to the rear under guard. A now familiar ritual occurred. A number of women came running out of houses and clung to their German boyfriends. They were of German, French, Italian and Dutch origin and protested with screams at being separated. We had discovered that many German units kept their women at the front with them. Only a few welcomed being 'rescued.'

One English-speaking prisoner, staring at our bright scarves and obviously speaking for many around him asked, "Who are you? Where did you come from?" and, "Who is the officer in the red turban?"

Jerry, without hesitation, pointed at Colonel King and growled, "That's the devil, and we're from hell."

THE RABBIT DRIVE

"Killing rabbits, killing Bosch, same thing. We don't win a gol-danged thing. They'll all be back. You mark my words." That was Uncle Ernest's blunt response to my asking him at dinner one night if he was going on the rabbit drive the next day. Uncle Ernest, who had fought in all of the major battles of the first World War, had refused to participate saying in his cranky way, "Darned foolish if you ask me. Just a waste of gunpowder and time. B'sides, you'll never get 'em all. Just the dumb ones and the babies. The smart ones hear the shootin' and stay in their holes. S'just another hair-brained scheme to sell a lot of cat'ridges and fill the motels in town. Scares the b'Jesus outa all the cows and horses. It's a dang-fool, hair-brained waste of time. That's what it is." My excitement about the drive had just taken a major hit.

During his tirade he had left the dinner table, washed his plate and silverware in the sink, dried them with a towel and put them in the cupboard. Then he headed for the back door, paused to say goodnight, thanked Mom for dinner and hoped I had a good time on the rabbit drive. All of this was said through clenched teeth. He closed the door deliberately, then rushed to the bunkhouse near the barn where he would spend the night. As often happened, he was his crankiest when his righteous indignation collided with his affection for us.

Later that night I drifted off to sleep sorting out what had happened. I knew that Uncle Ernest was often right about some things, but was usually so insulting that people would just gulp and ignore what he said. After Uncle Ernest had left, Dad reminded us of his brother's deep aversion to killing and shooting and said it was because of his war experiences. My brother, Herb, said that made sense to him. He told how whenever he asked Uncle Ernest to go hunting with him he would always say the same thing. "I'm finished huntin'. You just go on along." I went to sleep thinking that my Uncle's outbursts were kinda' like stepping on a puncture vine. It hurts, you pull it out, then it festers.

"Come on son, it's time to rise and shine. We've got just an hour to get ready for the rabbit drive." Dad was patting me on the shoulder as he sat on the edge of my bed, waiting for me to open my eyes. He had already awakened my brother Herb who usually required about three wake-up calls. I was easy. Whenever I woke up I was wide awake and talking. It was a family joke. Looking around my room, Dad said, "I'm always amazed at how much stuff you can cram into this room of yours."

Not wanting to give him time to tell me to clean it up, I asked, "Dad, will they really let me go on the line today, instead of working on the ammo truck or carting dead rabbits?"

"Yep, I think it will be O.K. You're supposed to be at least thirteen, but you'll be that in a week so nobody'll make a fuss." A sudden burst of laughter from the kitchen below my bedroom added to my excitement.

"Are Grandpa and Grandma up already?" I asked.

"They sure are," he answered, "Your Grandpa didn't want to miss the big shoot even though they got in pretty late last night from San Jose. They looked in on you but you were asleep. Your Uncle Vern and Aunt Hilda came down with them in their new Oldsmobile."

Herb came out of the bathroom at that point and after triggering our juke box in the hallway to play a Benny Goodman record, made a leaping dive from the door of my room to my bed and landed on top of me. I wrestled to get away while he dragged me out of bed onto the floor. Then triumphantly he said, "That's for letting Rusty into my room all the time." Dad was used to our wrestling so he just stepped out into the hallway and said, "Breakfast is about ready, boys. Better save your energy. There'll be a lot of walking today." As he headed for the stairs he added, "And get a move on. Our visitors can't wait to see you."

The Kingsburg Recorder, and even the Fresno Bee, had been carrying an announcement about our annual rabbit drive for several weeks now. The rabbit population in our part of the San Joaquin valley had exploded at an alarming rate. Entire fields of tender young grape vines and replacement vines were being devoured. In the latest issue there had been lots of information and even a map showing assembly points, area to be covered, and the finish line. It was recommended that ranches within the area be vacated for the day so no one would be in the fields or buildings. Outsiders from all over the state arrived in Kingsburg with their shotguns to sign up and participate on the firing line or to observe. Rifles were strictly forbidden. Their bullets traveled too far and didn't have the wide scatter of shotgun shells.

Extended family members timed visits to coincide with what was described by one writer as, "A unique opportunity to see what it was like for our boys on the front line in The Great War." My uncle Vern and my Grandpa Amos, who had tamed wild acreage in Idaho as a homesteader, often timed their visits from San Jose in order to join the drive. At breakfast, Uncle Vern was telling his latest jokes and paying more attention to Herb than to me, even though I laughed louder at his jokes than Herb did. Mom and Dad took turns flipping pancakes and pouring coffee, while Dad filled little spaces in the conversation by singing "Peg 'O My Heart, I Love You," and patting Mom on the fanny.

It was kind of embarrassing to have the only parents around who flirted with each other all the time, but it was kind of fun, too. Lots of my friends' parents didn't even talk to each other. Grandpa's elaborate savoring of the fresh buttermilk I had churned for him eased the slight I felt from Vern. It also helped to remember that Grandpa was a much better shot than Vern. Grandma Theresa was giving Grandpa the silent treatment for having sneaked some whiskey from his suitcase last night for "medicinal purposes." Grandpa's drinking was a poorly kept secret.

Pretty, vivacious aunt Hilda was in high spirits as she entertained with the latest healthy diet tips and managed to avoid any kitchen work. Mom, with her amazing ability to criticize with a compliment would say privately, "Hilda is the perfect *Guest*."

Mom was having a hard time with the rabbit drive. "I know they destroy our young vines but it seems so wrong to slaughter them this way." She also told her brother, Vern, that she didn't like it when he went deer hunting every year. She wasn't convincing on this though, because she loved the venison steaks he brought with him on visits.

Grandpa said he was glad that I would be on the shooting line with him this year. He reminded everyone that we had hunted together many times and that I knew how to conduct myself with a firearm. Herb said he planned to work on the rabbit detail picking up the dead ones after the firing line passed by. He would be collecting their tails for his Future Farmers of America club at high school. His class was having a contest to see who could kill the most animals and birds considered a hazard to crops. Mom announced that all of the women would be driving up to Fresno for a day of shopping and to take in a movie, since the drive would come right through our ranch.

As we got up from our pancake and lingenberry breakfast, Grandpa unlocked the gun rack at one end of our long kitchen and handed out shotguns. With a flourish and a smile he handed me a single-shot, twelve gauge, 'Monkey' Ward special that had belonged to Grandpa Anderson, my Dad's father. He said, "Bob, since this is your first time on the drive you get the best one in the lot. Besides, I've seen you shoot this one and you're a good match." Dad got the double-barreled Winchester and Vern had brought his own five-shot, ten gauge-repeater. Grandpa claimed the over-under, double-barreled Smith and Wesson for himself. Dad told everyone that Uncle Ernest, who had spent the night in the bunk house would be spending the day here, looking after the livestock, and would be with us for another night.

After making sure that all of our horses and cows were locked up in the barn or corrals, we loaded onto our Ford V8 Truck and drove the mile north to Clay School, where I was finishing the seventh grade. The road going east and west in front of the school was already busy with trucks and cars dropping off the hunters. The firing line would extend about two miles from the Kings river, toward the 99 Highway. Since everyone had been told to wear bright-colored shirts for safety, the road looked like the beginning of a circus parade. The hunters were soon lined up at about fifteen-foot intervals facing south. For the first time some women were in the line. Out-of-towners were greeting old friends with friendly insults and slaps on the back.

The ammunition truck that I had worked on for many years was decorated with red, white and blue bunting and streamers. It drove back and forth on the road selling boxes of shot-gun shells for about fifty cents a box. The truck would come in behind us on each road we passed, at half-mile intervals, to resupply anyone out of shells. Everyone on the line was reminding each other of the rules: Always keep your gun pointed down range; unload before leaving the firing line; when aiming at a rabbit, look beyond to what else you might hit before shooting; don't waste shells on "teases," the ones that run the full length of the line, just beyond range. You know when that happens because it sounds like a string of firecrackers going off as each hunter down the line takes a useless shot; stop shooting and give up if a rabbit tries to run between you; don't want you shooting each other; leave the dead rabbits for the pick-up boys following behind; if you run out of ammo, borrow from your neighbor and pay back at the next road; avoid bruises by holding the gun-butt snug against your shoulder as you fire; squeeze, don't jerk the trigger for better results.

A bugle sounded and a cheer rolled down the line as word was passed to move out. Scattered shots were heard all along the line almost immediately as the human rainbow of color stepped out into the fields. I couldn't wait for my first shot as I walked between Grandpa and my Dad. Vern was down a-ways with some old high school buddies, who were reminding him of the time they had pants'd him for dating senior class girls. They had run his pants up the flag-pole and tied him to the pole in his underwear. He was squirming a little but managed a grin. He liked telling jokes. He didn't like being one. Vern had lived with us and gone to high school when I was little. Just what I needed, another older brother. Suddenly everyone was laughing as we heard the string of firecrackers sound as a rabbit raced down toward us, just out of range. Grandpa spotted it coming and when it got close to his vineyard row he took a long lead, aimed high for the distance, pulled both triggers and dropped it. He accepted congratulations gracefully and quietly reloaded. It was then that I remembered something about Grandpa. He loved hunting and was a dead shot, but he was always sad and grumpy after he killed something. I realized that he and I were a lot alike in this way.

My first rabbit came straight at me between a row of vines and at about fifty feet I shot and was surprised as usual at the brutal recoil of the gun. Uncle Ernest was right. A twelve-gauge shotgun kicks like a mule. As the sound died down, I heard Dad say, "Good shot son. You got him." As we walked on by, catching up with the line, I tried not to look at it. It was easier if they were still, but I really hated the twitching and squealing. From then on I seemed to only hit about three rabbits every half mile and missed about twenty. Hundreds of rabbits were running all over the fields in great confusion, sometimes even in circles.

Grandpa grinned at me teasingly and said, "Bobby, I know you can shoot better than that. Looks to me like you're tryin' to miss. Like you're havin' fun just shootin'." I knew he was right, but I mumbled something about how hard it was to hit them when they were on the run. As I listened to the volleys of shots rolling up and down the line and inhaled the smoke from all the burned powder I felt exhilarated, but I couldn't wait for the drive to end. It occurred to me that if this powerful, organized firing line could just keep moving we could capture anything in our path. Without anyone shooting back, this was a very one-sided war. I knew that killing was deplored in our churchgoing community, but today it was not only acceptable, it was exciting. Several churches would be welcoming the hunters with free food and refreshments in town after the drive. A reward for the public service rendered.

We passed road after road, purchasing more shells and sometimes riding the truck to the next road to take a rest. It was always disturbing to see the trucks loaded with dead rabbits passing us on the same road with younger boys racing though the fields gathering up the dead rabbits and tossing them on the trucks. Dad joined me on one of these rides once and I said, "I wish we didn't have to kill them. I like seeing the rabbits running around our ranch, especially the cottontails."

He replied in a confiding tone, "I don't think we'll be having many more of these, Son. I'm thinking of a way we might wrap our vines in strong oil-paper so they can grow and the rabbits can't get to the buds. Some of the other ranchers are interested and we're going to give it a try. It might cost some, but I don't like this way of doing it either. Besides, it doesn't work."

After loading up on our truck which had been driven to the finish road, we passed on the celebration in town and went back to our ranch. Mom and Grandma had a chicken and dumpling dinner nearly ready. Aunt Hilda was busy watching. They were all wearing new dresses from Gottschalks and telling us about a Charlie Chaplin movie they had seen. Uncle Ernest had milked our two cows, fed the livestock and holed up in the bunk-house, saying he might join us for dinner. There was little talk of the drive. We cleaned our guns and locked them up. The news on our radio station KMJ reported that the Kingsburg rabbit drive had been very successful. Thousands of them had been killed and buried in an old sink hole near the city dump. Two cows had been shot but no horses. There were many bruises and black eyes. One hunter from Bakersfield had accidentally shot off a little toe while ducking under a wire in a vineyard. Herb announced that he had collected enough tails to win the F.F.A. contest.

Grandma, noticing my unusual quietness said, "What's wrong, Bob? Aren't you feeling well? I made chicken and dumplings especially for you and you've barely touched it."

"I'm sorry Gram," I protested. "I really love your dumplings. I just didn't have as much fun today as I thought I would. I keep thinking of all those rabbits in the trucks and I don't feel like eating. Maybe I can eat some later. Mom, can I be excused? I'd like to go outside for awhile. I think Uncle Ernest forgot to join us for dinner. I see his light on in the cabin so I think I'll take a plate of this out to him." Everyone thought this was a good idea. Vern was starting with another of his jokes as I left. I didn't want to hear it. I didn't feel like laughing. I just wanted to go out and be sad and grumpy with Uncle Ernest.

He saw me coming and said, "Come on in," before I even got to the screen door.

"Thought you might like some of Gram's chicken and dumplings," I said as I set the plate on a small knotty pine table. "It's real good but I didn't feel much like eating tonight."

"I'll try some, but my stomach's a mite touchy today too," he replied with an unusually soft tone.

"Were you here all day?" I asked.

"Yep. I had checks to write and this carn-sarned paper work to do."

"How was it having all that shooting coming at you when the drive came through here today?" I asked carefully.

"Didn't like it much."

"Did it sound like in the war?" Then something happened to my uncle that I had never seen before.

His voice choked up and cracked as he answered, "Yep, a lot like it, only these fools today weren't really trying to kill me like in France." Then he cleared his throat and hardened his voice to ask, "So how did you do on the drive today."

"Well, we killed a lot of rabbits," I began. "But—"

"They'll be back." he concluded.

"Well, it's not exactly that, Uncle Ernest. It's more that I really don't like killing things."

He pursed his lips, stared at the wall in front of him, nodded slowly and said, "I know."

A RIVER TOO FAR

Before leading us back into the troop truck convoy, Colonel King in a meeting with all of the officers and noncoms, informed us that our next objective was Eichstadt on the Altmuhl River and beyond that, Ingolstadt on the Danube. He said it was only thirty-five miles to the Danube but it would be a long trip. That was because several SS divisions were deeply entrenched in the villages and mountainous terrain along the way. Then he sped away to the head of the column pumping his arm up and down, the signal to move out fast. We were to ride until we were fired upon. He was wearing a wool knit cap and his red scarf was again around his neck and flapping in the wind behind him. The scalp injury was probably still too tender for his steel helmet.

The entire 86th division, as well as the 311th Combat Engineers, jammed all the roads leading south. Their trucks were filled with boats and inflatable pontoons. Tanks of the 14th Armored division were waiting for us on the edge of a field outside Wegscheld, where they were lobbing shells into the heavily defended town. As the tanks moved out to attack, our infantry units fell in behind each tank for protection. I was the operator in a radio jeep moving slowly between two tanks. As we entered the long wide field in front of the city, SS units in town opened up with everything they had. Artillery shells, mortar rounds, machine gun bullets and rifle fire descended on us with crushing intensity. Air support arrived in the form of a dozen P-38s followed by low altitude bombers who turned the city into flames.

The presence of the tanks was comforting until we saw the lead tank suffer a direct hit from an 88 artillery shell, explode and catch fire. Only one of the crew crawled out and he was in flames as he fell to the ground. The canvas tarp thrown over him was too late to save him. Then the order came for us to move out in front of the tanks and rush the city. I was now on foot with a walkie-talkie, leaving my jeep on the road with the driver who might pick me up later. As I ran past the tank trying to catch up with the company commander, I realized I would never get used to the smell of incinerated flesh. I also wondered who had given the order for us to become expendable and the rest of the tanks to be saved. We watched a fast moving, half-track reconnaissance vehicle mounted with two machine guns and a cannon attack the 88 position and silence it. It then moved against a cluster of machine gun nests and blew them up. By the time we caught up with the half-track on the edge of town, there was only one man left alive and he was bleeding from a hole in his neck. We sprinkled sulfa powder in his wound and left him for the medics. When we crawled into the bunker with the 88 that had hit our tank, we found the crew mangled and discovered that the gunner, now dead at the breach, was a very young woman.

I heard on my radio that one of our squads which had sped past us right into the city was surrounded. The second squad reported that six of the men had been captured with the squad leader, Marko. I relayed this to Captain Sullivan who hissed through his teeth, "We'll get 'em back! Let's get going. Fix Bayonets! Go!!" He led the way up the main street. I looked down at my bayonet and promised myself that I would never run out of ammunition and have to use that thing. I had never felt right about my bayonet work since being eliminated from the Expert Rifleman competition back in Camp San Luis Obispo.

It took five hours of vicious house to house fighting to chase the fanatical SS troopers from the town. After turning over prisoners to the MPs, most of us just collapsed into roadside gullies and went to sleep, assuming we might have a few hours reprieve. The familiar swelling in my jaw was back. My impacted wisdom tooth was acting up and throbbing with pain. My distraction with this was often mistaken as fearlessness, as I took extra chances, vaguely hoping to get hit and end the pain. I knew I couldn't go near the dentist and decided to steal some more morphine the first chance I got. Several of us made one last trip back into the town looking for our lost squad. We called out Marko's name and to our surprise got an answer.

"Hey, guys, don't shoot. These Krauts want to surrender," Marko announced in his Brooklyn accent. He emerged slowly from a collapsed basement leading a group of twenty SS troops with their hands on their helmets. The rest of his squad were on each side of the prisoners carrying burp guns and Mausers along with their M1s. He added, "They trapped us in an alley and after we surrendered they took us into that basement and kept us covered while they told us they wanted to surrender. Can you believe it? Anyway," he continued, "They wanted an absolute promise that they would not be killed before they put down their guns." Relishing his story now, Marko said, "I told them we were under strict orders to kill all SS and take no prisoners. Seemed to scare the hell out of them. Never heard an SS plead for his life before. When I heard you guys calling I told them it was safe and they almost threw their weapons at us." Marko told us that while they were waiting for the shooting to stop the Germans wanted to talk a lot. They had asked if we ever walked during combat, because they always saw us coming in trucks and jeeps. They had to walk everywhere. They had also said that they were just regular SS, not the bad kind, and that they hated Hitler. We were eager to add these new prisoners to the group preparing to march to the rear. Then we headed back to our roadside gullies. We were happy to have our buddies back. Marko kept us entertained wondering out loud if he was entitled to some POW pay for his four hours as a prisoner.

Even as the retreating German's continued shelling us, we slept between explosions. A greater worry sometimes was the sound of an incoming shell with no explosion. This meant either a delayed fuse or a dud. Both were given a wide berth because we never knew when they would go off. One such shell hit the road above me and skidded for almost a hundred yards before slipping off of the road and coming to a stop at my feet in the gully. I yelled a warning and we all moved to the gully on the other side of the road. I radioed the mine squad and marked the spot with one of my captured Nazi flags. Advance patrols reported booby-trapped roadblocks and pre-targeted roads, so Regimental Headquarters postponed our next attack until daylight. We sank into six hours of badly needed sleep. We bunched together in groups of three for warmth.

We were awakened on April 23rd to freezing temperatures by a now familiar chorus of husky, grinding sounds. Our trucks arrived again with orders to move us on to Eichstadt, about ten miles to the south. I was happy to ride in Captain Sullivan's jeep for my shift as radioman and as usual felt a surge of guilt at leaving my buddies on the truck. He announced casually, "We'll be crossing the Altmuhl River today. Do you know how to swim?"

I replied, "Yes I do, but won't the engineers have either bridges or boats for us?"

His cryptic reply was, "We'll see."

I sent and received messages all morning as the units ahead of us cleared many roadblocks. It was slow going because many of the barricades were booby trapped. Light shelling seemed to be hitting ineffectively over a large area. Soon we were approaching the river where the main bridges were destroyed by retreating Germans. Roger Langley, the chief radio operator, relieved me on the radio, and I became a rifleman again and joined the assault on a rear guard SS bunker on the banks of the river. The fire fight lasted about ten minutes and all of the Germans were killed. No one surrendered. I still couldn't understand how all those machine-gun bullets could go snapping by me so closely, day after day, without hitting me.

The engineers had moved in behind the rear guard and constructed a pontoon bridge across the river during the morning hours. As we moved up to cross, German 88s in the hills on the opposite side opened up a barrage on the bridge and completely destroyed it. The engineers immediately began constructing another one. In startling contrast to the war going on, the Altmuhl was calm and peaceful. Patrols were sent out to discover other means of crossing. One patrol found that we could actually walk across the old, bombed out concrete bridge and we were soon streaming into the city of Eichstadt. We operated more as a covert operation this time instead of an all-out attack, while we waited for reinforcements to come over on the pontoon bridge which was finished in late afternoon. Since the Germans were lightly scattered around town, we took isolated positions and functioned as snipers, just picking them off one by one as they appeared. Apparently the word spread that the town had been taken and most of the remaining troops had retreated or surrendered. The stragglers were our targets. I knew now why I had hated my sniper training back in the states. It was different fighting alone, more like cold blooded killing.

Suddenly a loud roar of voices echoed up the street punctuated with shouted greetings, in English. I rallied my squad and joining with other squads we went to investigate the sound and found a POW compound in the center of the city. Our trucks, having crossed the bridge, were rolling bumper to bumper through the city. We commandeered some of them and attached their winch cables to pull down fences and gates freeing hundreds of prisoners. They were mostly from the US, Canada and England and had been prisoners since the Tunisian campaign in North Africa two years before. We joined in their celebration and once again saw the majority of them race through the town looking for food and drink.

I had radioed Colonel King for Captain Sullivan that the city seemed secure in our sector and gave him the news about the POW camp and the Tunisian campaign prisoners. He came speeding up to the compound in his muddy jeep still wearing the shoulder holsters we had given him. As usual he was out of the jeep before it stopped. "God," he exploded as he walked up to us. "I always wondered if this day would come. On the radio you gave me the best news I've had in a long time. Corporal, are you sure there are guys in there from the North African campaign?" I said I was positive. "Then this has to be where my old friends are, and my outfit has rescued them. Damn, that makes me happy." Then, as Captain Sullivan walked over to use the radio in the Colonel's jeep, the Colonel pulled off the wool knit cap he was wearing. His head was still bandaged. I asked how his scalp was doing and he said, "You know, you and that musical medic probably saved my life when you sewed my scalp back on up in the Rhur. I'm grateful. I know you were screwed out of some college and a commission when they canceled A.S.T.P. Maybe when things calm down, I could recommend you to West Point. I'm a Goddam graduate you know."

"Thank you sir," I replied, "but I'm happy being a corporal and I just want to finish the war and go home. And honestly, I don't much like the odds against survival for officers in combat."

"Well, keep it in mind," he ordered. "And watch out for Brewster. He's bad news. Now come on with me while I see if I can find some old buddies." The closer we got to the prisoner compound the more excited he became. "I spent over a year in that desert hellhole," he explained grimly. "I learned a lot about fighting the Germans there, but lost a lot of men in the process." I didn't know quite what to say, so I just told him that my training at Fort Benning had been with veterans of the North African campaign and that we had great respect for them.

As Colonel King watched the allied prisoners milling around he spotted several he knew and called out to them. A first sergeant, a captain and a first lieutenant came running over and piled on top of the Colonel. Affectionate insults were exchanged through tears of joy as these former 'Lions of the Desert' cuffed each other around and became oblivious to everything else.

Since the city was crawling with thousands of released prisoners, as well as German prisoners, Colonel King ordered the Battalion to make camp in a forest on the edge of town. However, we were warned that we would pack up during the night and move on to Ingolstadt. Jerry and I pitched a tent together to escape the rain and sleet that began to fall. Many men just rolled up in their raincoats and threw their shelter-halves over them and went to sleep. Temperatures dropped below freezing and as much as we wanted to close the flaps of our two-man tent we remembered that we were still on the front line. I drew one shift as Corporal of the Guard during the night. I searched for ways to shut out thoughts of the men I had sniped today.

Jerry broke our silence, "What're you thinking about, Andy?"

"How I shoulda given those guys a chance to surrender."

"Jesus Christ, Andy, then they would have had a chance to get you. You forgettin' they were SS?"

"Yeah, I guess so. I was just tryin' to get all this shit out of my mind. I don't even remember how many I've killed, let alone wounded. Do you keep track, Jerry?"

"No, maybe fifteen or so—probably more. I just figure that for every one I kill, I'm probably saving a couple of our guys from them. Besides, I have extra reasons for wanting to kill SS."

"Yeah?

"Yeah, you remember that I'm Jewish, Andy?

"Yeah, so?"

"So the Germans hate us, especially the SS, and are locking up Jews in prison camps. I know that if you and I were captured by them, they would make you a POW but they would shoot me."

Shocked, I said, "Jerry, this is one of your cynical things, isn't it?"

"God, Andy, you are so naive. Where have you been? They have been out to get us for years. I see I'm going to have to give you an education—but not tonight. I need some sleep. Patton's got some real fun for us tomorrow."

"Hear those bombers up there ? When they get back to their base they'll have nice hot food and a bed to sleep in."

"Yeah, Andy and here we are sloppin' around in mud and blood. I hate 'em."

About ten minutes later, Jerry asked, "Andy, how do you turn it off—all this shit? I can't sleep. It's like I forgot how to do it, its been so long.

"I'm a good day-dreamer, Jerry. It got me in trouble in school but it sure helps here. Except when were in a fire-fight, I have to fill my mind with a good memory. Like when we dig in and take a break. That's when I dream. Otherwise I get scared and start shakin'. It's always good stuff, mostly about girls and my life on the ranch. I guess you could call 'em my foxhole fantasies. I try not to think about my family or Margie though, cause then I get soft and scared,—and worry about never seeing them again."

"Know what you mean. Girls work best for me too. I love thinkin' about gettin' laid. But you know me, I mostly think about the times I didn't. So what's your fantasy tonight, Andy."

"Well, I was laying here freezing to death and wishing I had a big thick blanket when I thought of something funny about my dog Rusty. He was the funniest dog we ever had and in the winter, he slept under a blanket. Funny stuff works too.

"O.K., tell me about it Andy. Sounds better than thinkin' about not gettin' laid."

RUSTY'S BLANKET

Our family dog, Rusty, always waited until our family was seated for breakfast before he left his cozy bed in the tank-house and sauntered up the steps to the porch in front of our kitchen window. We knew he had spent the cold winter night under a blanket of about eight cats, who fought for a warm spot on his sleeping form. As he crossed the porch, with the cats weaving themselves around his legs, he was gently tolerant and wore a smile as he stepped around them patiently. Glancing into the kitchen to make sure we were all present, he turned toward the two bar railing, raised up and put both front paws on the middle bar. "He's getting ready," I would say as the cats scrambled up to crouch in a row on the top rail, a two-by-four covered with scratch marks. Rusty looked down at the furry row of purring mounds and then out to the rows of grape vines which came almost to our porch. Disarmingly bored, he looked out to the high Sierras beyond the vineyards. In the bright early sunlight his usual reddish brown color became more golden, accenting his massive, muscular body. Pit Bull and Chow were the only comments on his parentage the day we bought him as a puppy for a dollar.

My brother Herbie jumped up at this point to wipe steam from our bay window so we could see better, as Rusty once more turned to us with his knowing grin. Then he buried his large, wrinkled forehead and nose into the underside of the cat directly in front of him. The cat, as if enjoying this display of affection, hunched up and leaned against him, purring so loudly we could hear it in the house. Then came the climax. While nuzzling the cat, Rusty jerked his head up suddenly, flipping it sprawling and screeching through the air, with its claws reaching futilely for the railing. He would watch until it landed in the soft dirt of the vineyard. Then he moved over slowly to the next unsuspecting cat and repeated his performance until one cat, in the midst of being launched, scratched his nose with a claw. He looked back at us, eyes drooping with embarrassed sadness as if realizing the game was now over. He nuzzled one more cat to wipe the blood from his nose then moved to the kitchen door for his reward, leftovers from the fridge and a pat on the head. We knew the cats would stay away from him today, but by tonight all would be forgiven, as they would once again be looking for a warm place to sleep and Rusty would welcome his blanket.

THE RED DANUBE

Ingolstadt on the Danube was our next objective and Captain Sullivan informed us that as of this moment, our 86th Division was out in front as the spearhead for the entire Third Army. Our Combat Team was supposed to be the second wave of our drive to cross the river. Our rolling armada contained as many captured German vehicles as our own. Except for the bristling weapons we were a close cousin to a gypsy caravan. Four towns were captured along the way without getting out of our vehicles. Trucks, jeeps and Volkswagens were used as if they were tanks. We always seemed to catch the Germans off-guard and before they had a chance to dig in and fortify. However, since we were dealing with SS troops, the fights were intense but brief. As the white flags came out and the hands went up in surrender, we began to realize that we had somehow become part of the leading edge of the assault. We didn't know who was behind us in reserve.

I was riding a captured German BMW motorcycle with a sidecar, as were many of my buddies, when we stopped for a "Take Ten." This was the infrequent toilet break when all vehicles stopped and a solid line of G.I.s in olive-drab overcoats formed along the roadside gully. Many were reading letters, munching 'K' rations, dozing or griping as they relieved themselves in unison. The line with its 'golden showers' extended for miles. As another part of this ritual, preassigned 'slit trench details' would have hopped down and quickly dug six-foot-long trenches about one foot deep and five inches wide, where those in need would quickly drop their pants and squat ingloriously over the narrow target for more serious relief. There was never any lingering as everyone dreaded being shot in that position. All trenches were quickly covered as we boarded our various vehicles.

A supply truck drove alongside our column collecting our back packs. We would carry only guns and ammunition in our attack on Ingolstadt. A tank column was speeding toward the city on a parallel road and we heard that Patton, himself, was leading the tanks. Our bombers and fighters came in low over our road and soon set fire to the entire city. The SS division in the city welcomed us with artillery barrages that were unrelenting. Out of the trucks and diving from one shell hole to another we filled the field with an entire battalion of men running at full speed, diving only when the screeching of 88s reached a low pitch, meaning they were very close. This time the tanks moved out into the field with us. We quickly grouped behind them and used a phone at the rear of the tank to direct the gunner's fire into the hot spots. I stayed close to the C.O. with my walkie-talkie, as we both realized that in spite of the tank protection we were taking casualties. The tanks, in the soft fields, were moving too slowly. After reporting this to Colonel King we received the crisp order to, "Forget the damn tanks, forget Patton and get the hell into the city as fast as possible. We're getting creamed." I relayed his message to all of the other company's walkie-talkies. A red flare would be the signal to resume our running attack. The tanks would cover us with continuous cannon fire until we reached the outskirts and the aerial attack would also stop then.

As the flare lit the sky we left the tanks and started running. Captain Sullivan stepped on a land mine and was blown about ten feet in the air. When he landed, both feet were gone and he was unconscious. I was blown off my feet and my helmet went about fifteen feet through the air. It landed in the pool of blood spilling out of the stomach of the new man, Rick. Three other members of my company were writhing on the ground with multiple wounds, moaning and screaming. Carlos, the other new man was dead, in an awkward sitting position with a hole between his eyes. Sullivan was dead and Lieutenant Kramer, our platoon leader, took over. I was so groggy from the concussion that every time I tried to stand up, I fell over. I just dragged myself around on the ground to the nearest wounded and met others doing the same. Marty, our ever-present medic, came over and checked us out and with his blessing, those of us not seriously wounded helped each other up and raced toward the city. Before he left, I talked him out of some morphine for my jaw. He stuck the needle in my neck and said I only needed a half a tube. Relief was immediate.

As we caught up with the line, we fired continuously at any flash of light we saw. We wrapped our scarves around our rifle barrels which had become too hot to hold and continued the assault all the way through the city. At a distance the SS troops were effective. When we were in their faces with bayonets pointed at them their hands went up in wide-eyed shock. We lost just one more man in the charge. I had forgotten my helmet and in one doorway, wrapped my scarf around my head like a turban to ward off the light, cold rain that began to fall. If a German didn't raise his hands immediately, he was dead. Frank Kraus of I and R was often the first to shoot surrendering Germans. He loved the bayonet as much as I hated it. We were wary of him because of his volatile temper and the fact that he carved notches on the stock of his rifle. He seemed to enjoy killing. I made a decision to stop counting how many German soldiers I had shot.

Halfway through the city, the remnants of my squad and I were racing through a side alley and came face to face with a full squad of Germans, all kneeling with burp guns aimed at us. They had us, and we started to lay down our rifles to raise our arms. As the SS officer smirked at us a familiar, friendly voice called down from a window in a southern drawl, "Well now, I'm mighty glad to have you in my outfit." Chester, thinking that the Germans were new prisoners, was extending his usual greeting. Startled, our would-be captors all looked up to see Chester, all smiles, holding a machine gun. In that pause, we raised our rifles and began firing. Chester, correcting his original take on the situation, opened up with his machine gun and finished off the squad. When he came down to join us he was apologetic, but when we said he had rescued us he brightened and said, "Wa'll, you know, I allus' like to he'p out." We told him he was going to get a bronze star. We would see to it. Then Chester handed me my helmet which he had picked up and somehow washed off in a shell hole full of rain water.

When we finished our charging race through the city, we were suddenly on the banks of the Danube. We had collected hundreds of prisoners whom we turned over to the mop-up units following us. The Germans had blown all the bridges and the battalion on our left was getting ready to launch small landing boats to cross the Danube. Even with all the action going on I heard myself muttering in amazement, "I'll be damned, it isn't blue at all, its green." We were to wait until the engineers put up a footbridge on small pontoons. Other engineers further downstream were constructing a vehicle bridge which was under steady artillery fire. We heard later that it took five attempts before they got a bridge completed.

The foot bridge took too long, so my company went across in small boats. Bullets and shrapnel from artillery and mortars ripped through the wooden sides and by the time we got close to the other shore, we were half full of water and sinking. We dropped the ramp and waded in water, chest deep, to the opposite bank. Machine gun bullets churned the water all around us. I had always felt lucky to have missed the D-Day landing but now it felt as if I hadn't. Men were floating in the water and lying in crumpled piles on the bank. I saw intestines and an arm floating in the water along with toilet paper rolls and letters from home. Magnesium flares on parachutes made us even easier targets. In the glare of the flares the water was now red, and the bank was slick with bloody mud.

Lieutenant Kramer was shouting, "Move on, leave the wounded for the medics." I couldn't resist pulling at least one man out of the water and onto the beach. In the growing darkness, I decided to give him several quick pushes on his back to pump out water in case he was still alive. He coughed, sputtered and turned over. It was corporal Brewster. He looked at me in disbelief and I moved on. I could feel myself bleeding under my clothes from pieces of shrapnel and wondered when there would be time to pull them out. I joined the rush up the bank and looked down into the long line of trenches and machine guns. The SS defenders were quick to surrender but from the screams down the line I knew that some of my buddies had decided to take no prisoners and that Frank was busy with his bayonet. Although the temptation was strong to do the same I still could not shoot someone with his hands up.

We bivouacked in a field beyond the Danube where trucks arrived with hot food, supplies, ammunition and our field packs. We slept, ate, welcomed in April 27th and ate every chicken in sight for a day and a half. We were still the front line of attack and our patrols kept the Germans off balance. I now had time to pull out the pieces of shrapnel, including splinters and pieces of rock, and add them to the collection in my pocket. After my trip to the aid station I was covered with bandages. A number of men were sent to the rear with serious wounds. Mine were not.

Colonel King gave the order to move due south on a road that would take us to Munich through a bunch of little villages and into Austria, through the Alps. Our own version of a Blitzkrieg captured the towns of Gaden, Geisenfeld, Wolzack, Gembach and Eschelbock in quick succession. In one town we were stopped in our tracks. It was perched on a two hundred foot cliff and the only access road was heavily fortified. Impatient with this obstruction, Colonel King radioed orders for our battalion to spread out in frontal assault position, charge to the cliff and then scale it. We were certain that our hero, King, had "lost it." Yes, we had trained for this at Camp San Luis Obispo and climbed some cliffs but this looked impossible. We had no ropes or climbing gear. It would just be foot and toe holds. On his flare signal we started toward the town in great despair. The enemy knew we were coming and pinned us down almost immediately. I could see the Colonel in his jeep in the center of our line, wearing his helmet again. When he saw us pinned down, he stood up in his jeep, ripped off his helmet and smashed it onto the ground. His driver dutifully picked it up without getting out of the jeep. Then King was staring intently through his binoculars. Suddenly he sat down and the jeep lurched forward dodging explosions and shell holes, heading straight for the cliff in a high speed zig-zag course. He stopped safely at the base of the wall where he radioed back the welcome orders. "Withdraw to the woods on the north side of town. Blacken faces and clean your weapons. We've got a surprise for them tonight." The sigh of relief was unanimous along the line as we crawled to the forest and slept the rest of the day.

The sky cleared and in fairly bright moonlight, about midnight, we followed King in single file along the edge of the forest to the bottom of the cliff and then along a foot path to his discovery. He had found not only an opening in the rock wall, but the six-inch thick door was open. We walked through a winding, musty tunnel with darkened flashlights looking carefully for demolition charges, but found none. The tunnel led upwards to an empty building, on the city square. Eventually when everyone was in, the Colonel said, "Now, let's go get them. Use surprise. Try not to shoot unless absolutely necessary."

We spread out into all of the streets, surprising Germans on guard, or strolling the streets with girlfriends, or in bed with them. Within an hour we had the town, without a shot fired, and over two thousand SS prisoners. We transferred the prisoners to our relief battalion and went looking for our trucks which soon lined the streets. As we passed Colonel King in his jeep on our way out, he shouted out to us with a big smile on his face, "Great night for hunting."

DETOUR TO DACHAU

On our rush toward Munich we were slowed briefly by fortifications on the banks of the Isar River, which we quickly overpowered and loaded into assault boats once again to capture the other bank. Still on foot, we marched toward the Isar Canal where we expected another boat crossing. However, a small artillery spotter plane saw what appeared to be a tunnel under the canal off to our right. The pilot landed right on our battlefield and ran up shouting for us to follow him. Lt. Kramer, now company commander, joined the pilot and we all followed in company strength. It was a tunnel, and it was dry and intact but also had demolition charges strung at intervals along the top edge. We cut the connecting wires as we filed through the passage still expecting that the Jerries would blow us up at any minute with the charges that were left, or suddenly drown us with a flood of water.

We were able to exit on the other side but were immediately saturated with enemy fire. We exchanged fire across an open field until engineers cleared the tunnel of all debris and two entire regiments were able to run through. With the signal to attack the town we poured out into the field at full speed. The entire garrison of four thousand surrendered. As we separated the prisoners and isolated the officers we found many Luftwaffe pilots, who had been sent to the infantry because there was no gasoline for their planes. Our trucks had found an intact bridge downstream and were ready for boarding on the outskirts of town. The rides were now very brief but a welcome opportunity for a little rest. As we rode off talking about our conquest, we weren't particularly concerned that none of us knew the name of the town.

It was April 28th and we were just a few miles from the outskirts of Munich when we pulled into a forest to wait for our bombers and fighters to pound it into rubble. While finding our rest spots in the forest, we all noticed a strange smell in the air. Between drizzles we found the sky was full of gray ash which settled on our helmets, shoulders and packs like fine snow. We had experienced ash fallout from burning towns before, but this was somehow different. The smell was sickening. Lieutenant Kramer tried to settle the mystery by telling us that it was obviously from the bombing of Munich. Then he sent a patrol back to check out a peaceful looking farm we had seen as we entered our wooded bivouac area. He wanted to make sure there were no snipers waiting to sneak up on us. The patrol leader soon sent up a flare calling for help. Many of us went running back ready for a fight. The patrol was staring into a barn and also pointing rifles at a farm couple who were on their knees, pleading for their lives. Four men, stripped of their clothes and wearing dog-tags were lying dead on the dirt floor. They had been executed with single shots to the backs of their heads. Frederick, who spoke some German, said six SS soldiers had ambushed a jeep with four GIs , took their clothes, shot them in the barn, dressed in their combat gear and drove off in the jeep. The couple had been told their daughter in the house would be raped and killed if they made any trouble. Amazingly, they had written down the serial number of the jeep and referred to the SS as murderers. I think that saved their lives, as we were wanting to kill someone for this. Reluctantly, we left them and I put in a call for M.P.s and our intelligence unit, G-2.

On returning to our forest, a heavy, cold rain began to fall. We formed one man tents for ourselves with our ponchos or shelter halves. The rubber and canvas mounds seethed with silent fury. Not since the Ruhr campaign a couple of weeks before had combat felt so personally devastating. All around our impromptu camp we could hear a chorus of zip, zip sounds as we sharpened our trench knives hoping for an opportunity to use them soon in close combat.

"Corporal Anderson! Where the hell are you?" The rain, pelting my helmet had lulled me into my dream world. My trench knife and whet stone were still clutched in my hands. First sergeant Bruno's harsh voice jarred me awake, ready to kill.

"I'm over here, Sarge," I shouted back as I tried to get my cold, stiff legs under me to stand up.

"A telephone line to Battalion headquarters is out. Take the jeep with the wire reel on it and a couple of men and fix it." He explained that the line ran along the road to some little town called Dachau. He told us to stay out of the town, because some big deal was happening there tomorrow and that we had no contact with first battalion on our right flank without a phone line. He added that all the walkie-talkies were broken. Sarge was always harsh and cutting but he was angry now, cursing the officers holding up his field commission.

I found Jerry and Frank Kraus, and we three headed where the Sarge had pointed. With a flashlight and blackout headlights on our jeep, we followed the telephone line that had been laid for about a mile alongside the road to where it just ended. We kept driving knowing that sometimes kids or German patrols would cut out lengths of wire to make repairs difficult.

In the dark, progress was slow but soon we passed a city limit sign reading "Dachau." I had missed the turn to Munich and knew I was supposed to turn back but drove on, until I veered off into the outskirts of the town just as the sky was beginning to lighten. Jerry tapped me on the shoulder and said, "Andy, let's get the hell out of here. We're not supposed to be here."

Still reeling under the influence of yesterday's atrocity I shrugged off caution in favor of recklessness and said, "Let's see what's in those buildings up ahead and then we'll go." It looked like a compound of some sort and the main building was right in front of us. The other guys seemed to share my belligerent mood.

Kraus summed it up with, "Fuck it, fuck the sarge, let's kill some Krauts."

Jerry said, "I see some fencing over to the left, I'll bet it's another POW camp." We left the jeep out of sight and raced up to the two story building and finding the door open went in and found no one there. It was an office with desks, chairs, pictures on the wall and file cabinets in side rooms. Papers were all over the place. Someone had left in a hurry. With burp guns and Thompson submachine guns at the ready, we left the rear of the building ready for a fight. No one was there. We now saw more wire fences and empty guard towers. We came upon some barrack type buildings and Jerry muttered, "Just like Camp Livingston. Damn, I wish I had more clips for this fucking burp gun." Creeping in the shadows of very early daybreak we tried to open doors to the buildings but they were all locked.

An SS guard came calmly around a corner with a rifle over his shoulder and instantly raised his arms. Surprised but not shocked he said in understandable English, "So you're here already. I wish to be a prisoner of war. You must not kill me. We knew you were coming today. I stayed to surrender." I asked who was in the camp still thinking it might be a military base or POW camp. He replied, "This is a prison, not a camp."

"Who are the prisoners?" I asked.

"Undesirables," he replied with an expression of disgust. "There are no Americans." We ordered him to open a door to a barrack. He said he would not. Frank put a knife to his throat and drew blood. The door was quickly opened. The scene that greeted us was too horrible for our numbed minds to comprehend. We stepped into a room crowded with closely packed tiers of wooden bunks, with men wearing thin and faded striped prison uniforms that looked like pajamas. Some were still sleeping, some were sitting on their bunks and some getting up to greet us. Some, we discovered were dead. The unmistakable smell of gangrene, that I knew of from buddies with frostbite, overpowered the suffocating odors of urine and feces.

"Holy Shit," Kraus exploded. "What the hell is going on here." We were all well acquainted with death but not with this kind of living death.

The men moving toward us had been starved until their skin was tightly stretched over their bones and skulls. They were covered with sores and open, bleeding cracks in dry skin. Their heads were shaved and it was difficult to imagine any blood flowing in their veins. They were so yellow. Some just stared at us vacantly in disbelief, and others moved toward us slowly with boney arms outstretched and with smiles that cracked skin and looked ghoulish. One man with sunken eyes and smile reached out with both shrunken arms to welcome me with an appreciative hug. He smelled of urine and rotting flesh. I froze in terror as my stomach exploded all over his feet. Jerry recovered first and was shaking hands gently with the men as he sputtered at me, "Jesus Christ, Andy, couldn't you have waited a little."

The man accepted my apology and while cleaning his feet with a bucket of water spoke to Jerry in Yiddish and Hebrew. "This is where Jews are brought to be killed," he explained in a dry, hoarse voice. "Also, gypsies, homosexuals and anyone opposing Hitler," he added. "See, I told you, Andy," Jerry exploded.

With my outrage seeping through my shock, I asked, "Do you mean they starve you to death?"

"Yes," he answered through Jerry, "They also beat us to death, hang us and shoot us out on the firing range. Then they burn us in the crematorium." He was exhausted and could talk no more.

Kraus, speaking German, found that the prisoners had seen our bombers and heard the battle coming closer and expected us Yanks today, the 29th. He learned that most of the SS guards had fled but that some were still here. In the distance we could hear the unmistakable sounds of tanks and not knowing whose they were, we decided to get the hell out of there. At that point our SS prisoner bolted for the door but Jerry caught him and quickly cut his throat and pushed him out into the yard with blood spurting all over the place. Numbness gave way to a new feeling, hatred. I wanted to kill everybody responsible for what I had seen.

We quickly tore 'K' rations out of our packs and handed them to various men, then ran out into the yard and along the row of buildings using the guard's keys to open the doors and moved on. Running around a long, high wall, I stumbled over what appeared to be a stack of logs. Then I discovered I was lying on top of a stack of stiff, dead bodies piled against a wall. Kraus pulled me up and whispered that it looked like an execution wall, from all of the bullet holes and blood on the stucco.

Fog had rolled in, dimming the early dawn and we heard the screeching, clanking of tank tracks approaching. Maybe they were ours and maybe they were German. We tried to find our way back out of the maze of huts and buildings. Hearing some German soldiers coming we dived through a door into a building with a large smoking chimney. "Must be the Crematorium," I gasped and then looking up we saw three bodies hanging from ropes above a kind of scaffold. They had been better fed, but were dead. My flashlight revealed another stack of bodies near the furnaces. I ripped open an oven door with my entrenching tool and saw the remains of several partially cremated bodies still smoldering. The gas had been turned off. Now I knew where the smell and ashes had been coming from.

Jerry said it for me, "The bastards were trying to get rid of the evidence." Hardly speaking we all raced out of the building, headed in the wrong direction and came to an electric fence, with a moat in front. Racing now to beat the morning light, we kept on until we came to a row of railroad cars with one door partially open. Legs and arms were hanging out and the men women and children jammed inside were all dead. "Probably starved or suffocated," Jerry snarled.

"I've had enough. Let's go kill some SS," sputtered our volatile Kraus. At that moment, I was glad he was with us. He loved to kill Germans. We spread out and raced back across the darker part of the yard to the main building where we had entered. One by one guards appeared as they heard our running and we shot them. One guard, dropped his Mauser and raised his hands but Kraus shot him anyway. In the administration building, I paused to rip a saw-toothed, eighteen inch dagger off of the wall and stuck it into my cartridge belt. The tanks were closer and we could even hear shouting and shooting.

We found our jeep and were back on the road making a pact that we would not speak of what we had done for fear of being court-martialed. Jerry couldn't resist saying, "It's the only way, Andy. The last thing you need is another court-martial. Besides, those people will be out of there today. I'm sure those were our tanks we heard." We stayed off of the main road to avoid patrols that would be looking for the stolen jeep with Germans in GI uniforms. Riding in gloomy silence we couldn't find words to express what we had just seen. We found the other end of the telephone wire. Now, in the early daylight we could see that a fifty foot piece had been cut out. We spun out a fifty foot length of phone wire and spliced it in and checked with a field phone to make sure it was now working.

Off in the yard of a farmhouse we saw a woman hanging out laundry. We drove over and found she was hanging her clothes on our missing telephone wire. With our approach, and spotting our telephone reel, she was on her knees pleading for her life. Jerry asked her if she knew what was going on in the Dachau camp. She said, "It is a prison for criminals, but they are not all bad. Some of them have worked on our farms around here." Jerry told her what we had seen and she promptly collapsed, assuming we were going to kill her. It had crossed our minds but instead we jumped in our jeep and took off.

On a side road leading back to our bivouac area we came upon corporal Brewster and a driver, stuck in a mud hole. They had been on courier duty until the line was fixed. The driver threw us a chain which we hooked to our trailer hitch and pulled them out. I was about to drive off when Brewster came running over, red-faced and outraged. "If you ever help me again, I'm going to kill you, you son-of-a-bitch." That was it. I'd had it. The nightmare I had just experienced exploded in a killing rage. I vaulted out of the jeep and grabbed Brewster by his pack straps.

I pulled his puffy, red face up close to mine and yelled, "Brewster, you stupid little prick. Do you think I would do anything to help you, you worthless piece of shit? You aren't worth helping. You're not even worth killing. You're worse than these fucking Nazis. I wish I'd let you drown in the Danube. I already beat the shit out of you once and I can't wait to do it again."

Jerry had come around the jeep and put a hand carefully on my shoulder saying, gently, "Andy, take it easy! You might kill him." Kraus was still sitting in the jeep grinning expectantly. Brewster seemed to have stopped breathing and turned pale.

Then he spun away toward his jeep saying, "Fuck this shit, lets get out of here." Everyone breathed again as they drove off.

Jerry muttered, "Jesus Christ, Andy, now your really going to have to watch him. You just humiliated the shit out of him." I said I didn't care and if I had another opportunity in a fire fight, I would nail him.

Kraus, no longer smiling said, "I'd be happy to do it for you."

Back in the forest, Sergeant Bruno, wearing his lieutenant's bars even though the order had not come through, shot out his rude greeting. "Where the hell you been, Andy? Took you long enough to fix a broken line."

With Brewster lurking in the background, but close enough to hear, I said coldly, "You know how it is Sarge. I ran into some shit in the dark." He stared at me for a second and then decided to leave me alone.

Our trucks were late, but the morning was used for a hot meal served up by our cooks and for cleaning up a little. I spent some time with our supply sergeant, Bob Hartley, in the supply truck, repairing weapons and helping him hand out replacement equipment for which the men signed a 'statement of charges.' This allowed the army to deduct the cost of lost equipment from our next paycheck. I had always considered him a friend, ever since he got me my job as company armorer and my corporals rating after my court-martial with Colonel King.

Our officers were busy writing letters to families of our latest casualties and Chester was making the rounds, happily distributing mail. As usual, I handed him a couple of my old letters as he gave me my new ones. Even though working with Hartley always calmed me down a lot, I still felt a gnawing fury in my guts and decided not to read any letters from home. I didn't want the confusion of mixing the two worlds right then. I wanted to kill more Germans. I wanted to kill Brewster. The images of the prisoners in that camp, the stacks of shrunken corpses and the furnaces kept racing through my mind. I knew that Kraus, Jerry and Mike were probably going through the same thing. Even though we could hear tanks and gunfire in the direction of Dachau I wanted to be certain that somebody knew what was going on there. Maybe I should tell Lieutenant Kramer.

Just then, Colonel King came through and ordered a company formation. In a bellowing tone of outrage he told us about the concentration camp at Dachau and that it had just been captured by elements of the 7th Army on our right flank. He said it was a "death camp" and just one of many such places, where mainly Jews were imprisoned. He confirmed that the smell and ashes all around us were from bodies being burned in crematorium ovens. Thousands of starving prisoners had been released and SS troops in town had been rounded up and locked into the barracks. Guards found in camp had been executed. Townspeople were being forced to walk through the camp and help bury the stacks of dead bodies. The Mayor of the town had been killed. Other such camps had been liberated and more of them were on our route south and east. Some prisoners had reported a group of GIs wearing Blackhawk insignia had entered the camp at daybreak. King said he informed Regimental Headquarters that his men had been under strict orders to not enter the town and that they did not disobey orders. First Sergeant Bruno was glaring at me as King finished his announcement, but shrugged his shoulders and walked off as we were dismissed to board our trucks. I thought he figured I would tell the truth if he asked me if we had gone into Dachau against orders and just didn't want the trouble that would follow. It might jeopardize his field commission.

Back on our trucks, we were soon on our way past Dachau, heading for Munich. We saw many other combat units moving in different directions. It was a military traffic jam. We had time to compare rumors with guys walking along the roads or in vehicles. Everyone seemed to know about Dachau. Some of them had been among the first in and reeled off descriptions of the concentration camp. No, it had not been a dream. They too had seen the starving prisoners, the crematorium, the stacks of bodies and the train load of dead men, women and children. I felt a cold hard knot of hate in my chest and the line blurred between German soldiers and civilians. They were all guilty. They should pay. I wanted to kill. Especially the SS. They were in charge of Dachau and apparently other places like it.

We on the truck were as one in our outrage. We promised to take no more SS prisoners. Kraus said, "Just give them to me. I'll take care of them." One guy with a 7th Army patch on his shoulder said he had helped execute some SS guards. Frank threw him a package of Old Gold cigarettes and nodded his approval. Not one person was reading mail from home as we inched along in our convoy. I needed to resolve something in this cold, bloody, inhuman hell first. I could not begin to understand the magnitude of the evil I had experienced.

So much anger was brewing we were mostly silent, avoiding all of our usual teasing and banter. Moving slowly through the congestion, I noticed columns of Japanese GIs and learned that they were part of the Japanese regiment, the 442nd. They all had 'the look,' as we called it. The weary, vacant stare of eyes that have seen too much. Bodies sagging from too much pain and not enough rest, moved automatically, each in a separate world. I rallied myself out of my stupor enough to remember that I had lifelong friends from Kingsburg in the 442nd. I looked up and down the columns yelling, "Gila River," over and over. There was a chorus of, "Yo's." I wasn't surprised. That's where most of my Japanese friends were sent after Pearl Harbor, when they and their families were re-located to camps away from the west coast. Many of them had joined the 442nd to fight in North Africa, Italy and Europe. "I'm from Kingsburg--in the San Joaquin Valley--ever hear of it?"

"Yeah, Swede town," someone yelled back. "Knew some people at Gila from there."

"Do you know Hideyo Yamada or George Matsuoka? They're in your outfit."

"Yeah, George bought it right after Normandy and Hideyo caught shrapnel for the third time. He's in a hospital somewhere."

I told him that Hideyo was one of my best friends in high school. Conversation ended as we moved in opposite directions. I had managed one last stupid question, "How you guys doin'?"

"Pretty good—only four hundred percent casualties so far." Then he added, "But it beats the hell outa that god-damned concentration camp they put us in at Gila." Suddenly my rage about Dachau collided with a guilty helplessness I still felt about doing nothing to stop the imprisonment of my Japanese friends. My body responded with a throbbing headache and swollen wisdom tooth as we moved into the country .

A TOWN DIVIDED

My cousin Sheldon's radio voice was strained and lacking its usual breezy style as he interrupted the playing of Glen Miller's "A String of Pearls" to announce, as if asking a question, "Everyone of Japanese ancestry is to be evacuated to re-location centers immediately?" My cousin, the chief engineer and first disc-jockey at Fresno's radio station, KFRE, was clearly shaken as he read off a list of compulsory registration locations. In disbelief, he blurted out, "This can't be true." After a pause, he moved ahead to report the news. He emphasized the word "unsubstantiated," as he read a bulletin on acts of espionage and sabotage in the San Joaquin Valley, leading to the searching of Japanese homes and the seizure of cameras and radios. Our little farming community of Kingsburg, with its large Japanese population, was still reeling from the attack on Pearl Harbor and from the fact that we were actually at war with Japan. We believed an attack on California might come soon. Young men were rushing to enlist in various services, as we struggled to know how the draft would work, what rationing would mean and when we would enter the war with Germany.

Gloom settled over our normally boisterous breakfast table. Mom and Dad exchanged a look that I knew meant something really bad was happening. In the past that look was a moment of intimate unity between my folks that always made me feel safe. Until now, I had believed that my Dad and Mom could fix anything, solve any problem, and help anyone in need. Now, though, at sixteen and a half, I could feel their shared dismay and it was as if the late December frost blanketing the vineyard outside our bay window had knifed into our warm, steamy kitchen with an icy chill. My twenty-year-old brother Herb, a student at Reedley Community College who had already enlisted in the Marines, spoke first. "It doesn't seem fair," he protested. "What if Sweden went to war with the U.S.? Dad's Swedish and Bob has a ham radio station. We'd all be taken away!"

I was thinking only of my Japanese friends. "What about Kazuto and Kijos and Yurico and Shizuko and Hideyo and Minoro?" I asked, "I've known them all my life. What will happen to them? Their families aren't traitors!"

My Dad, who didn't pretend to have answers when he didn't, said thoughtfully, "No, of course they're not and it doesn't seem fair to me either. I don't know what will happen. A lot of people haven't made friends with the Japanese the way we have, and they will believe their allegiance is to their homeland."

Herb said, "Since Pearl Harbor, my classes with Japanese students in them have been very awkward. They are very quiet and won't look at us. My friend, Ki, told me he was ashamed of Japan's attack and said that he could see the hostility and blame in most of our faces." My brother, who seldom lost his temper, slammed his fork down and said, "I didn't know what to say because I knew it was true. All I did was tell him not everybody felt that way, although I knew most of the non-Japanese students had been looking away and avoiding eye contact in the hallways and even in the classrooms. He just grinned at me and said, 'You're different Herb. We've been best friends since the first grade.' And you know folks," Herb whispered as he stared at the table with his head in both hands. "The worst thing is, I think I've been different with them too."

To make my brother feel better and also to relieve my own guilt, I said, "It's the same at high school, Bud, but I didn't see it the way you did. Since December 7th, the Japanese kids weren't as friendly, didn't say hello sometimes, just looked at the floor when we passed, hung out more together and spoke Japanese to each other, something they would never do before. I thought they didn't like me anymore. But then I got kinda' suspicious. I thought maybe they were for Japan and could turn against us if Japan invades. Now I feel terrible. I hadn't realized that they must be embarrassed—and scared. I wish they would say more so I could know what they're thinking."

Herb said, "Give 'em a chance, Bud, you talk enough for everybody."

Mom smoothed a wrinkle in our blue and white, checkered tablecloth as she said she hadn't realized that was going on at school. "You boys have always been so close with your friends. We adults have always been friendly but more formal with each other." Then she added, "I've been dreaming about an invasion and I don't honestly know how our Japanese neighbors would react if they were face to face with Japanese soldiers who might be relatives. You know how they have always kept such close ties with their families in Japan. Many of the women in my church group have already decided they can't be trusted." Her voice grew thin and quivery as she revealed her fear of standing up to them even though she knew they were wrong to prejudge that way.

Dad reached for the coffee pot from the stove behind him without getting up and refilled our cups as he put his arm around her shoulder. Then he said, "It's been hard enough to sort this out but now, with this relocation business, it's going to get a lot worse. I just hope the government knows what it's doing. It's hard to believe that they do though because they're telling us that we can't trust our friends, and that seems wrong."

We all agreed that we had never had any reason to distrust the loyalty of our Japanese neighbors and friends. We would try harder to be natural and as outgoing as we had in the past, but we wondered how could they trust us. We were caught in a sickening whirlpool of confusion. The wrenching struggle between our belief in government infallibility on the one hand, and our trust in proven lifetime friendships on the other, made it impossible for us to be natural. How could they not feel our ambivalence as distrust?

As the youngest member of the family, I sat with my back to the bay window now coated with steam. I suddenly found myself jumping up and wiping off the steam with a towel so we could see the Matsuoka ranch on our left and the Yamada ranch on our right. We all gazed at the harmonious interlacing of our ranches, just above the row of dozing cats on the porch railing and just below the dense tule fog about twelve feet off of the ground. I could see the veins standing out on Dad's temples and a redness at the top of his ears. Mom was swallowing a lot and teasing a piece of bacon on her plate. Herb was trying to balance on the back legs of his chair. Mom sighed, "Things will never be the same," as we all left the table to face a community about to be torn apart. I raced off to catch the bus for school, eager to be natural with my friends who were about to be ripped from their homes, friends, schools, possessions and freedom, and sent to internment camps.

Even George Henderson, my bus driver and typing teacher, looked disturbed when he pulled up in front of our ranch. I could see immediately that most of my Japanese friends were not on the bus. Yoshaki, who got on at the next stop, looked around tentatively, then as I moved over to make room he sat next to me. With only two other Japanese students on the bus, there was an unusual absence of camaraderie. Everyone was quiet. As we settled into silence I found myself looking forward to my civics class where our unconventional teacher, Mrs. Gunnerson, would open up a discussion on this morning's news. But then, remembering my resolve at breakfast, I decided not to wait until my third period class and asked Yoshaki if he had heard the news. He said, "We were listening to Sheldon this morning and afterwards we got two phone calls from people in town telling us to go back to Japan where we belong."

"Do you know who they were?' I asked indignantly. "Let's go talk to John Croft, the Police Chief during lunch time today," I continued, suddenly feeling very warm, even in the cold bus. "They can't do that!"

Trying to calm me down he spoke in a soft, even tone. "Thank you anyway, Bob, but it would only make things worse for us, and everybody. We must be polite and not call extra attention to ourselves. If we protest it will make people angrier and then we might be in more danger. There are many in our town now that see us as the enemy and as you know, they all have guns."

Deflated, I asked, "Well, then, what are you going to do about this relocation stuff?"

"What we have been ordered to do," he continued calmly. "We'll find somebody to run our ranch until we come back, then store or sell nearly everything else. We can't take much with us. Just a couple of suitcases."

Mr. Henderson brought the big, yellow rattle-trap of a bus to a screeching final stop before reaching school. Four kids got on, including one of my best friends, Hideyo Yamada. Hideyo and I had gotten to be friends through our many hours spent in after-school detention. He, for talking too much, and me, for not paying attention, not sitting still, talking too much and for being obsessed with Barbara and Florence. We also played pranks on teachers, and had locked the ill-tempered custodian in the gym towel room. That was good for a week's detention. Because of his small size and agility Hideyo was the star of our tumbling team, scrambling to the top of a three-story pyramid. This morning, his usual mischievous smile was missing. In fact he was scowling. "Good morning, Mr. Henderson. You gotta write me an excuse for first period, cause we're gonna be late—and I'm freezing my butt off, waiting."

Our white-haired bus driver, noted for his wisdom, passed off the rudeness, smiled, and said gently, "Hideyo, if you just stomp that barnyard mud off of your shoes you can get on and I'll explain why we're late." Then above the whine of the old Chevy engine and stripping the gears as usual he shouted, "I had to finish listening to Sheldon's news broadcast this morning and got so upset I got a late start. Then I waited a little extra at each stop for kids who didn't show up; I don't blame them though, for wanting to skip school today. In fact I didn't want to go to school today either."

At school, Mr. Henderson swung the bus in a large arc and joined the line of unloading buses. All of the buses were late but no one seemed to mind. As we all spilled out onto the asphalt parking area I noticed many of the absent riders waiting in groups for their respective buses to arrive. They had been driven to school by their parents. I spotted Tom and Mary, who like many of my classmates had taken American names. As brother and sister, they lived with their family on a fruit ranch near ours. They were my earliest playmates. Anticipating my question they explained their absence on the bus this morning as we walked to our classes. "Our parents wanted to protect us from being ostracized on the bus," Mary began. "They thought it might be easier at school with more people around. We feel great shame about what Japan has done. We feel betrayed and attacked---as you do, by the homeland of our ancestors and relatives."

Tom interrupted, "But **this** is our new home, and the only home Mary and I have known. We are Japanese, but we are Americans. But people no longer believe it. Now we're betrayed by America also. We're being sent away and we've done nothing wrong. You've seen how nobody talks to us on the bus, except you, and Bobby Harris— and Jeanette." I was saved a helpless response as they slipped into their classrooms. I said I would see them in our civics class this afternoon as their doors closed. I headed on to the music room for my first period, band practice, where Mr. Schwartz made it clear it would be business as usual.

With my problematic ability to do two or three things at once, I strapped on my street drum and played well-memorized rhythms for an hour, while my mind stayed with my Japanese friends and their families. Did the F.B.I. really know things we didn't know? They were supposed to! Are they really going to lock up all Japanese families because a few aren't loyal? Has anybody been arrested yet for a crime? Sheldon says no. I wanted to yell at somebody, but Yoshaki said that will make it worse for them. Is he right? Uncle Ernest says they can't be trusted because they stay to themselves, eat strange food, take baths together and are always polite. But Uncle Ernest doesn't trust anybody. The parents seem to be accepting the orders to get ready to leave. Does that mean they are guilty, or ashamed,—or smart.

I was sure they were at least very scared. Hideyo showed me a letter about the relocation stating that it was for their own protection. I thought there might be some truth in that. Two Japanese barns had been burned and somebody had shot a rifle into a Japanese home. I began to feel dizzy and tried to shut off my thoughts by paying attention to the music, a Sousa March. It was a relief to be pounding something. In fact, the entire marching band was playing louder than usual. It was an even greater relief when our leader decided we would hit the street and practice marching up through town.

In my next class I noticed that most of the Japanese students were present and hard at work. I found myself just staring at my chemistry book, but I was really quietly studying each of them, trying to guess what they might be thinking and feeling. I had grown up with these kids sharing classes, sports, national holidays and the fruit harvest, but they seldom shared their feelings. Then again, neither did many of my Caucasian friends. Then I realized it was anger they didn't express, except for Hideyo. They **were** polite and they were good students. Much better than I was. The only Japanese kid I ever saw get in trouble at school was Hideyo and that was probably because he was with me. Whenever I asked any of them about being so good, they simply said they were raised very strictly.

At this point, Mr. Ewan, one of my favorite teachers said he noticed that I hadn't turned a page and hadn't moved for about twenty minutes and wondered if I needed help. He knew of my problem with concentration, so with the unusual focus on my chemistry book for so long, he knew something was wrong. He seemed to know how to reach us. In fact, earlier this year he had asked the school board for money, for me to construct a school radio station as motivation and a kind of therapy for me. I thanked him and said, "I guess I was daydreaming." I liked his crooked, understanding smile but my mind went right back to my Japanese friends. But now I turned a page once in awhile.

I thought of how so many people, in town especially, were upset by the differences in how they lived and did things, but I found those differences intriguing. For instance they went to Japanese schools on Saturday. At the age of seven I wanted to go too, to learn Japanese and more about Japan, but my parents convinced me that it just wasn't done. Some went to Buddhist churches and some had joined Christian churches in town. I had learned a lot about their customs, food and other family routines when Tom and Mary's family had worked for us and lived in a little foreman's house on our ranch. That was before my Dad helped them buy their own ranch in their children's names. Parents who were born in Japan were not allowed to own land.

A fish truck would come once or twice a week. I would run out to the see all the fish in a giant ice box on the back of a pickup. It was fun to watch the bargaining, just like my Mom at a rummage sale. When the Matsuoka's bought lobsters or crabs, I would hang around until they were cooked and plead with Tom and Mary to show me how to eat the meat out of a bright red joint with chop sticks. I liked it better than candy. Rice and fish rolled in seaweed and fishcakes were also special treats. Steaming bowls of sukiyaki filled with chicken, noodles and many vegetables would often be delivered to our kitchen door with smiles and bows, especially when there was illness in the family. We, in turn, shared beef and poultry from periodic slaughters.

Bowing became a natural part of our greeting with adults, once Dad explained that it was an expression of friendship and respect, like tipping our hat or shaking hands. It was not subservience. While we kids were often in and out of each other's houses, we went to our own homes for meals. An unspoken boundary provided that we would share food but not our tables. Another boundary existed about cross-dating. In spite of the camaraderie that existed and the many things we shared, it just wasn't done. It wasn't talked about. That's just the way it was. The Japanese family bathtub was a source of great curiosity for me, but a thorn in the side of the conservative keepers of morality in our community who considered nudity evil. A minister in one of our churches once referred to it as a pagan rite that should be abolished. Little did he know that his daughter was a regular at our nighttime ritual of 'skinny dipping' at a sacred petting place called 'second drop.' Once, when we were about nine I had said to Tom, enviously, "It must be fun to see your sisters naked on bath nights." I had also asked if they ever had guests on bath night.

He had replied patiently, "Sorry Bobby, you can't come. It's a family thing. We're used to each other and it's kind of a sacred, traditional thing. We've seen each other without clothes our whole life, and we know how we are different and it's not a big thing."

Not particularly comforted, I had said, "Well, I still think you're lucky," and wished I had a sister.

After Chemistry, Algebra and Spanish I raced to my Civics class, eager for the wisdom of Mrs. Gunnerson. She immediately referred to the relocation announcement and tried to provoke reactions and discussion. We were all scared and afraid we might say the wrong thing and antagonize each other. She read announcements in the Fresno Bee and stated her opinion that our government was over-reacting.

Shizuko, a year older than I and an honor student stood up and as if speaking for all Japanese in the class said, "Discussion is useless. It has all been decided. There is nothing anyone can do. There are not enough people of good feeling for us to stay, even if we could. The hatred and prejudice is growing. We have all been getting phone calls and letters telling us to leave. We no longer know who our real friends are."

I squirmed at that and interrupted her to say, **"Some** of us are real friends."

She smiled warmly and replied, "Bobby, you are like a brother and we grew up together, but not many people feel close to us or care what happens to us." There were some audible "No's" and groans from some of my caucasian friends but we knew it was useless to disagree.

We had all become aware of escalating anti-Japanese feelings and the 'shunning' that followed Pearl Harbor. Differences were no longer accepted, but were being talked about openly with exaggerations and fear verging on paranoia, especially among the adults. Assumptions had been made out of ignorance and misinformation. In stores and on the sidewalks in Kingsburg pros and cons were argued loudly or agreed upon quietly. Among friends and within families the re-location issue produced intense feelings and conflict. It seemed to me that those in favor were the most vocal. I was stunned by the stupidity of some of the arguments for the Japanese internment, so clearly anchored in personal bias. For the first time in my life I really understood the meaning and danger of racial prejudice. I could not even begin to understand the magnitude of the damage that would be caused by this government order and plan. Our class discussion shifted to sharing of information about the specifics of what was happening.

Army troops would be dispersed to facilitate the orderly removal of Japanese families from the San Joaquin Valley. They were to be given no assistance in disposing of their homes, vehicles and possessions. They could take only what they could carry and board a Southern Pacific Train which ran through town, to a processing center. From there they would be taken by Army Trucks and trains to internment camps for the duration of the war with Japan. Departure dates would be staggered over the next few weeks. Only with gentle insistence of our teacher did our Japanese friends share this information. Some of them pulled government letters out of their pockets and read excerpts to us. Outspoken Jack Schaeffer, wrestling with the same angry helplessness most of us felt exploded indignantly, "Aren't you angry? What if you just don't go? I'm leaving for the Navy in June but that's what I **want** to do. If I didn't, they would have to come and drag me out."

Shizuko, again speaking for the group, answered with her now, grating calmness, "It is not our way to be angry or to defy our government. Your government is our government and it has spoken. We will obey. And besides, they **are** coming to drag us out."

Jack, one of our best athletes, was stymied for a moment, but then he fired his parting shot. "I hate when you guys say, 'It's not our way, or it's just our way.' Can't you change some things? Look at me, I used to be a loud-mouthed jerk, and look at how much I've changed." Jack's reward was the only ripple of laughter in class today. Even he saw the humor in this as he replied, "Well, O.K., maybe I haven't changed so much. I'm just upset. I'm about to lose a lot of friends and teammates. Without you guys our school sports are going to be a farce."

From that day on a sense of unreality deepened in all of our lives. Japanese kids began to drop out of school to help their families prepare to leave. Some of them let us know when they were leaving and others just seemed to disappear with their families, without goodbyes, on late night trains out of town. The few references made by some teachers in classes at school were sympathetic over-simplifications, implying that the painful disruption of the relocation of the Japanese was a necessary, but tragic, consequence of the war. This attitude grew stronger as Japan began the conquest of islands and countries in the South Pacific and as Kingsburg boys became casualties.

The time pressure on Japanese families to dispose of virtually everything brought out the best and the worst in my neighbors. Some ranchers, like my father, became overseers for Japanese ranches with powers of attorney to make all decisions with no change in ownership. Others moved in to gobble up the ranches with quiet claim deeds for a small fraction of their worth.

Hideyo's and Johnny's families were among the last to leave and they remained in school and in all school activities until the last minute. They were both involved in our Junior class play, 'Sorry, Wrong Number' as stage hands. One day the entire cast was driving around the countryside in Morrey's flatbed truck, picking up furniture from our various homes for our stage set. We were about to cross the railroad track at the head of main street when Hideyo yelled out to stop. He explained that it was against the law for him to cross over to the west side of the tracks. I had not heard of the arbitrary dividing line which was to keep the Japanese further away from the coast line a hundred miles away, so they could not help the invading Japanese army. He jumped down and sat on a railroad track until we came back and picked him up. He greeted us with a satisfied smirk as he announced sarcastically that he had only had time to pull the spikes out of two hundred yards of rails. To celebrate the absurdity of the law and before returning to school, we drove over to one of the two Japanese stores alongside the railroad tracks where we all bought shaved ice snowcones. The only place in town that sold them. The owners were very gracious and apologized for having just lime flavor left. We tried not to notice a pile of suitcases near the front door. The shelves were nearly empty. Hideyo said they were scheduled to leave in two days. The store would be locked up and left. They had found no one to buy it or take care of it.

As the departures continued, it was no longer a topic of conversation. A resigned acceptance calmed the agonizing rupture in our little town. There was a bizarre matter-of-factness now about the steady flow of Japanese families leaving each day from the ancient train station. The families seemed not to want people to see them off. Putting myself in their shoes, I began to understand this. While we felt we were saying goodbye to friends we cared about, I saw how they might see the farewell as our being in agreement with those who were taking them away. They could easily be thinking, *Well, if you care so much, why are you letting this happen.*

In my helplessness and timidity I began to know shame in a way that made it hard for me to look at them directly. The farewells were somber and quick. It was the same with Hideyo, who was about the last to go. We shook hands as he wished me luck in the class play. He said, "Bob, you should stay with Florence,—you look like you really enjoy the kissing scene in the play." Then as he climbed on board the train he turned on the top step and said, "Hey spook, I'm really going to miss you, and detention."

I said bleakly, "I can't believe you're really leaving." Then, while trying to control the shake in my voice I managed to say, "I'm so sorry about all this."

He snapped back with, "Now don't get sappy on me Bob. Just make sure you answer my letters. Besides, as soon as I'm eighteen I'm going to volunteer for the service. I'll probably see you in combat somewhere. And oh, by the way, with all of us gone you'll probably make the first team in something for a change." He deliberately bumped into an armed M.P. as he bolted onto the landing of the railroad car to join his family. Huge clouds of steam and smoke wrapped around the departing train, closing the curtain on Hideyo's elaborate and mocking apology to the M.P.

One week later, somebody burned down the Japanese store, and I made first string on the basketball team. A year and a half later, I was drafted into the Army and Hideyo enlisted in the all-Japanese, 442nd Infantry Regiment in Europe.

Before the Japanese internment

PRISONERS

Our convoy rolled through more Bavarian towns on our way to Munich, which was under heavy air attack by our bombers. It was April 30th when we went through the city, following several armored divisions. The SS division occupying the city had retreated due east to Erding, where they dug in for a fight. We heard that the 101st Airborne division had made the first pass through and then headed straight for Hitler's Eagle's Nest at Berchtesgaden. Streets were filled with slippery mud and buildings were still collapsing as we drove through. The tank column preceding us had cleared a path for our trucks with their tankdozers. While we were stopped briefly, a sniper shot our Big Mike right through the heart. As he lurched forward clutching his chest, Kraus and I fired at the muzzle flash simultaneously, and the shooter pitched forward from his third floor window onto a pile of rubble on the street. Mike was not breathing and had no pulse. We decided to keep him on the floor between us until we could flag down an ambulance.

We stayed on the trucks until we left Munich on a dirt road headed east toward Erding. During a stop, I was assigned to drive a medical officer in a jeep, pulling a small trailer filled with medical supplies. I found it difficult to keep up with the fast pace of the convoy on the slippery road. Visibility was also bad due to the heavy mist in the air. I could feel the trailer sliding around behind me and pushing my jeep whenever I put on the brakes. With the throttle down as we went over a hill, I suddenly saw a row of taillights right in front of me, now moving very slowly. The damn convoy had almost stopped. I hit the brakes to avoid crashing into a truck and slid off of the road. The trailer, with its own momentum, jack-knifed, came unhooked from the jeep and flipped over, spilling medical supplies all over the road. We got out to inspect the mess while I apologized to the Doc for the accident.

He poked around in the mess while I waited for him to explode. Instead he said calmly, "Oh well, fuck it. Let's get going." As he climbed nonchalantly back into the jeep I noticed a box of morphine capsules and slipped a handful of them into my overcoat pocket. We blended back into the convoy without our trailer and I felt a great sense of relief. As soon as no one was around I would inject some morphine into my swollen cheek. I knew that half a tube would stop the pain and I wouldn't feel so drunk.

We sailed through town after town until reaching Erding on May 1. This was the third day since leaving Dachau and we were aching for a fight. Colonel King had driven along the entire convoy announcing that we would keep the "god-damn Krauts on the run." He stopped at the truck I was again riding and upon noticing that Jerry had lost his yellow scarf said, "You're out of uniform, soldier." Jerry pulled a bright green negligée from his jacket and waved it around as King grinned saying, "That's more like it." We flagged an ambulance and lifted Mike into it. He had died instantly and had a kind of smile on his face. I hoped when my turn came it would be quick like that. Then we chased the retreating Germans. We often had them in sight and when they did stop and try to resist we jumped off of our trucks and ran right through their positions before they could dig in, often with captured burp guns. Curiously, we discovered that our relentless attack was rewarded with fewer casualties.

Since meeting with the 442nd and hearing about my Japanese friends, I had lost my resolve to take no prisoners unless they were slow to get their hands up. On this day we killed more than we captured. In one town, when four SS troops came striding out of a building waving white flags high over their heads, Kraus quickly volunteered to take them to the rear. He returned much too soon without them. Later that day someone reported finding four dead Krauts in the woods. They had all been bayoneted. Just two days before I probably would have helped Kraus.

Rumors were flying that the German Army was in full retreat in the south. This was not the case at Erding. All hell broke loose as we faced one of our worst battles. Pinned down, Colonel King called for all the artillery available. The city was saturated with shells until the fanatical SS began to surrender. Three hours later we had taken the entire city and in the afternoon our Regiment had captured an adjoining airfield intact. Thousands of prisoners were sent marching to the rear under light guard. Many had surrendered in fairly large groups and we began to see something new. When we would surround our prisoners, we would find they had shot their SS officers who refused to surrender. We soon learned to ask, "SS?" when taking a group. In an instant, the regular soldiers would move away from SS officers and point at them. They would often smile in satisfaction and encourage us to shoot them. We would then find where the SS lightning bolt insignias had been removed from their collars. I was surprised at how many prisoners spoke English.

With no rest, we assembled by companies and were told by Lt. Kramer that we were now leaving Patton's 3rd Army and had become part of General Patch's 7th Army. It was May 3rd, and our entire 86th Division was to move up into the Austrian Alps and down into Austria. We captured town after town traveling through one forest after another. A hot meal and sleep seemed to be ancient memories. The weather was colder than ever. While stopping in one forest to refuel the vehicles, our mess truck appeared out of nowhere and within a half hour were dishing up hot food into our mess kits. The kitchen crew had also set up a canvas Lister bag filled with purified water for filling our canteens.

Orders were relayed that we would stay put for the rest of the day and send out patrols to see what the Germans were doing. Each patrol came back with twenty five or thirty prisoners and no casualties. It was the same with the patrol I led into a very dense part of the forest. We stumbled upon two squads of Germans just sitting in a clearing with their rifles across their laps. They immediately raised their hands and pointed to three SS officers that they had obviously shot. One man spoke English very well and said they had been trying to figure out how to surrender. The officers had killed some of their men who tried to surrender. This man was actually a lieutenant and was eager to talk. He said, "We are of the Wehrmacht, or regular army, like you. We hate Hitler and think he is insane." Speaking for others in his group he said they all just wanted to go home to wives, family and children. Many had already lost family in the bombings. Although my hatred had cooled, we were only five days away from Dachau and I thought how easy it would be to just kill these guys and leave them in the forest to rot. I hated it that I felt some sympathy for them. They really weren't like the arrogant, machine-like SS.

"What about Dachau?" I found myself shouting. "How could you let that happen? What about all the other concentration camps? Why are you surrendering now? It took you long enough to decide you hate Hitler. You just know that you've lost. That's why your surrendering, just to save your god-damned necks. Why did you decide just today to kill your officers? Why didn't you do it before?" The officer translated everything I said and all smiles disappeared. *They aren't so sure now that we won't kill them*, I thought. Good. Let them squirm.

Then the officer said, "Corporal, we don't have good answers to most of your questions, but we don't know about Dachau or concentration camps. We just know there is a prison farm near Dachau." I found myself starting to believe them until I realized they were probably just trying to save their lives. Still, we hustled them up and herded them back to our camp where they joined our other prisoners.

We now had about two hundred prisoners in a dense forest as night fell. No one wanted to take the prisoners to the rear. While debating this I drew a large square in the clearing and ordered them to stay within the lines. I announced matter-of-factly that they would be shot if they crossed the line. We handed out 'K' rations and they rolled up in their blankets and coats for the night. The forest around us was full of the sounds of movement. Rain clouds blocked out any moonlight, so we built a campfire near the prisoners and changed guards throughout the night. We sat close to the prisoners as a protection from snipers in the forest. The English-speaking prisoner and four others had moved closer to my position and wanted to talk.

They had all been drafted from small German villages, hated Hitler but felt powerless against his followers. They fought to save their own lives and had lost most of their friends. They had said goodbye to many Jewish friends, did not believe the rumors about the concentration camps, and loved what was left of their families. My cynicism about their powerlessness began to weaken at the reference to saying goodbye to Jewish friends.

I recalled my own helplessness and shame at the train station in Kingsburg when I said goodbye to many Japanese friends being taken to relocation camps. I remembered a required lecture at Fort Benning on the 'Psychology of Hate,' justifying the killing of the enemy. I thought it was stupid. With a strong feeling of revulsion I thought of my fellow guard Kraus, who loved killing, and knew I was not like him even though I wasn't so sure a few days ago. Most of my vengeance was gone and the welcome numbness returned.

The lieutenant said he had one more thing to tell me. "There are many more soldiers in the forest who want to surrender but are afraid they will be shot."

At first light, a prisoner head count revealed a new total of almost five hundred. This seemed to confirm what the prisoner had said. They wanted to surrender safely and had slipped into the group during the night. As the day brightened and while waiting for marching orders, Jerry, J.C. and I borrowed medic's helmets with the red-crosses on them and walked out to the surrounding woods. Feeling absolutely naked without my rifle and certain I had been set up to be killed by the prisoner's suggestion, I was shocked and relieved when about two hundred Germans came rushing out of the woods with their hands up. By evening we had over a thousand. Our officers were not pleased with this extra complication as we were to move up into the Alps at any time.

Against all prevailing G.I. wisdom and my brother Herb's advice, I volunteered to take them to the rear prisoner compound myself. With food almost gone and nothing for the prisoners, I left immediately in a Jeep mounted with a fifty caliber machine gun and Jerry riding shotgun. Another dark night descended on us as we led the column of prisoners about five miles to the rear through dense forest. As a swirling misty rain fell we could hear only the prisoners footsteps above the purring of the jeep engine. How easy it would be for them to overpower us as they followed the tail-lights of the jeep. How easily they could slip away into the forest. At the compound I handed in a report vouching for one thousand, one hundred and twenty eight prisoners. The guards counted over three thousand. The walk through the forest had tripled the number. Before leaving the compound with its many fires burning, I saw prisoners throwing all of their belongings onto the ground to be searched. I scooped up some Iron Crosses, Luger pistols, an SS dress cap and a couple of dress swords, boxed them in a 'K' ration carton and stowed them on the supply truck with my repair supplies.

Traveling again through the dense forest and with Jerry dozing in the seat beside me, I wondered if any wires were strung across the road at neck height. Then I remembered that this jeep had been equipped with an improvised, goose neck wire cutter attached to the front bumper. I thought of my childhood fear of the dark and my father assuring me that the sounds of chains holding horses in their stalls and dragging across feed troughs were not the sounds of soldiers marching as I had imagined. I blessed the numbness that had returned. We arrived at the clearing before daybreak and fell asleep in the jeep. I had brought back a supply of 'K' and 'C' rations so the day was spent eating and preparing to move over the mountains that night. I would be the operator in the radio jeep, with our communications officer, Lieutenant Houston, riding along. Chester made the rounds wishing us all a happy "Cinco de Mayo." It was May 5th, about the time that my folks would hearing from the Hernandez family about their arrival date to harvest our peach crop.

SURRENDER

As we descended on the treacherous, winding road of the Austrian Alps in a column of jeeps and trucks and German vehicles of every kind, die-hard Germans opened up on us with 88's and mortars. We kept moving in the darkness, pushing damaged or destroyed vehicles over the sheer cliff. A shell exploded on the roadside above us and our driver was hit with shrapnel. The jeep came to a stop against the embankment. We removed the driver, who was still alive, and left him to wait for the ambulance. I gave him a shot of morphine from one of the tubes in my pocket and took over the driving.

About ten minutes later another shell exploded on the upper embankment, very close to us, blasting the jeep onto its right side and over the side of the cliff. Lt. Houston disappeared with the jeep along with my helmet and rifle. I was thrown onto a bush on the edge of the road. I had grabbed a handful of thin branches of the bush with one hand. With my body dangling into the black void, I searched with my free hand for something more substantial to hold onto. I succeeded only in dislodging a landslide of small rocks. There was nothing else within reach so I grabbed another handful of branches. Icy rainwater from the road poured over me. I could feel both hands slowly slipping. The bush itself began to loosen in the soggy dirt as some roots began to show. I yelled for help, but my voice was lost in the roar of passing truck engines and exploding shells. I knew that those behind us assumed we all went over the cliff. My fingers were becoming numb. My grip was weakening. I knew that in a matter of minutes I would join all of my equipment in the canyon below. My thoughts were racing. I *hate falling, except for the swan dives into a stack of hay at home. When I fall, I'll pretend I'm doing that. What will I feel when I hit? Will I die quickly? After all the bullets and shrapnel I dodged, I'm going to die in a god-damned mud hole. Will anybody ever find me? I wish I had my pistol, I could shoot myself on the way down. What will my family do when they get the news?*

An angry voice crashed through the maze of my thoughts, as two pairs of hands grabbed each of my wrists and dragged me back onto the road. "Ah shit, it's you," crackled corporal Brewster, as he slammed his helmet into the road in disbelief. "I can't believe I just saved your sorry-ass life. If I'd known it was you I 'da let you drop."

Brian, the other man, and our newest replacement, got me a blanket and helped me move to the rear of their jeep. He said he had just happened to see my hands in the headlights. I sat in front of the exhaust shivering and began to thaw out as the convoy rolled by. Brewster started to walk away. Then he paused and stared at me with the venomous look that had followed me since our fight at Camp Livingston. Remarkably, his eyes softened as a pleasant thought crossed his mind. He shared it immediately.

"I just decided that we're even. You saved my life and I saved yours. Now, you uppity son-of-a-bitch, just stay out of my way." With that, he jumped in the jeep, saying he would wait for Brian over the next hill and that he had to get outa' there.

Still wet but warmer, I thanked Brian for the rescue and said I would wait for another radio jeep to come along, so he took off walking along the edge of the road to catch up with Brewster. I was amazed that Brewster seemed to have forgotten that I was going to kill him. While waiting and watching Brian walk up the hill in the dim lights of the convoy, I saw him blown into the air as I was knocked flat by the blast. He had stepped on a land mine.

The column stopped as several men on the passing truck were injured by the blast. I raced up the road to find him moaning and lying in a bloody heap on the shoulder of the road. He was riddled with fragments. His legs were twisted together like a bloody rag doll. Bones were sticking out through his shredded clothes. I gave him a full tube of morphine and covered him with blankets that were thrown to us. I sat down on the road next to him and lifted his head onto my lap.

Marty came running. "Aw shit," he said. "He just got here." As our eyes met, he shook his head then stuck him with morphine. I didn't even tell him I had already given him some. Then he went back down the road looking for an ambulance.

Brian was gasping for air and coughing up blood. He was pleading, "Corporal,I...can't... do this...I know...I'm going. Please...please...shoot me. Oh, God...," he moaned, "...it hurts too much,...please...." He had managed to reach his pistol but couldn't lift it.

I said, "O.K.."

I reassured him, as I felt his blood warming my lap. Making sure no one was watching, I took the pistol out of his hand, put it to his temple and released the safety. Before I could pull the trigger he heaved a long sigh and stopped breathing.

After the ambulance arrived to pick him up, I found an abandoned German motorcycle along the road and after disconnecting a 'screaming mimi' booby-trap, I fired it up and rejoined the convoy. Burning vehicles lighted much of the hillside and made us easier targets. For an army that wanted to give up they were sure giving us hell. At one point the terrain provided us protection from the bombardment and a halt was called until morning. I dried my clothes on the warm hoods of trucks, while I sat on the motorcycle wearing just an overcoat. I kept the engine running to stay warm until my clothes were ready. Then I rolled up in my overcoat and poncho raincoat and passed out, waking at daybreak covered with three inches of snow.

Colonel King came sliding up to us in his jeep. As usual, he was standing up in the passenger side, wearing an even brighter red scarf. Shouting so all could hear, he informed us that we were to move out immediately and continue our attack down the Alps for a drive southeast through Austria. First Sergeant Bruno was finally given a field commission to Second Lieutenant, as a groan of dismay rippled through our assembled company. Although he was now an 'officer and a gentleman,' we continued to call him "Sarge." He responded with deflated glares.

Colonel King announced that Chester, our company clerk, had been awarded the bronze star for single-handedly rescuing my squad when we were captured in Ingolstadt. We all cheered as Chester hid under his poncho. Then, as his jeep leaped into action, King yelled, "Let's go finish this damn war." As our caravan moved out through the slushy snow, the sun broke through the perpetually gray sky. For the first time we could see the majesty of the Alps. The early morning sun reflected off of patches of snow, as we were all silenced by the vastness and sheer beauty of what had become our fortress for the night. We raced for the green valley below. When my BMW motorcycle ran out of gas I just pushed it over the cliff and climbed into a radio jeep that stopped for me. Shelling was light and sporadic. I found comfort in looking down the winding road below to see our tank corps leading the attack for a change. From the stack of captured weapons on our salvage truck I had picked up two burp guns taken from prisoners and dead bodies. They were ideal for our close combat way of fighting.

In spite of periodic shelling from die-hard artillery batteries, most of us reached the valley below, where my regiment captured four towns and villages with white flags flying and almost no resistance. As we followed our tank column into one of the towns we were led right into another concentration camp. We raced into the camp on foot, tearing off locks and doors and executing the few remaining German soldiers we could find. Although we found no ovens this time, there were again, stacks of emaciated bodies. The starving prisoners in various striped uniforms were smiling and shouting greetings in many languages. We gave away all of our rations again and shook many boney hands. Men, woman and children crowded around us crying. A very young boy grabbed me around one leg and wouldn't let go. I walked around a bit with him standing on my boot and attached to my leg, until two women pried him loose, saying I had to go and kill more of their guards. I didn't even know the name of the camp. We were ordered to move on quickly, as special supply trucks and personnel arrived to take charge.

Amazingly, many of the prisoners formed columns along with us as we moved out of the town. They wanted to help find and kill more Germans. From then on, the endless refugee lines choking every road included many freed or escaped prisoners. We were now in Austria, heading toward Salzburg.

In the third town we slowed down to search each building. A high ranking general was supposed to be hiding in one of these towns. As our company moved through the town we found only frightened families who seemed happy to see us. A man who said he was from 'H' company came jogging up to me as I came out of one building and asked if we were missing anybody. I said I didn't think so, but he wanted to show me something. On the way up the street he said he had found this guy, who had been killed by a woman who said he had raped her. Said he had told the woman to get the hell out of there fast. When we entered the building, it was now empty except for Brewster, lying dead in a pool of blood on the bedroom floor. I told the 'H' company man that Brewster was ours, and in unspoken agreement we left him where he was. Then we leaned his helmet and rifle against the front of the building and parted company, leaving the mess for the Graves Detail.

When I caught up with my squad Jerry said, "Find anybody, Andy?" "No, not really," I answered. "Just Brewster. He's dead."

Jerry, his large eyes rounder than usual asked, "Andy,…did you?"

"No Jerry, the son-of-a-bitch was dead when I found him."

The next day, May 6th, as we approached Pischelsdorf, we were greeted by three German officers with a bed-sheet on a long pole. The officers wanted to surrender an entire regiment waiting in the town. While Colonel King was negotiating this, we were instructed to dig in for awhile in a nearby forest. I dug a very deep fox-hole beside the radio jeep so I could hear the radio. I took the microphone in the hole with me. I finally decided to read my stack of letters. Margie sent pictures of herself in a sexy, flimsy negligée and a letter to match. Mom's and Dad's warm, conversational letters melted my protective numbness. I couldn't wait to see them and try to forget all of this. I didn't want them to know that I had actually killed people. I would write later. We had been on the attack so long there had been no time to write.

Then I found what I had been waiting for. A letter from the hospital in Le Havre. The letter, sent as army mail, had "Danny, of the 101st Airborne," as the sender's name. She wrote as she spoke, her own special mixture of French and English. She had received the necklace and was delighted. Her mother had taken it to a jeweler friend who told them it had eight diamonds on it. She said she would never sell it. Her brother had been captured by the Nazis, but was liberated by American G.I.s. Most of the Airbone casualties had left the hospital, replaced by the wounded from the Ruhr Pocket. She was glad I had survived that battle. She missed me and hoped to see me before I went home after the war. A patient in the hospital had addressed and mailed the letter. She too, would never forget our last night together. After reading these letters I found myself more vigilant than ever. My fatalism evaporated. I was more determined than ever to stay alive.

About mid-afternoon there was a light bombardment from another mountain ridge as the latest German prisoners were marched past us to the rear. There was an unusual quiet for a long time. Radio messages were routine. "Sugar four king three—any action?"

My answer was "No, all's quiet." Then, while eating the dinner version of a 'K' ration, the radio came alive.

Call letters were skipped as the excited voice announced "Cease fire--cease fire, the Germans have surrendered."

I was sure I was dreaming or had misunderstood, so I crawled out of my hole and into the jeep and asked for the message in Morse code. I wrote down the message, one word at a time and ran with it to the command tent, yelling all the way, "The war's over, the war's over." Later, messages advised caution as planes appeared, dropping leaflets with the news for any troops on either side who might have been cut off from communication.

The sounds of distant gunfire gradually diminished. The sudden release from the constant threat of death took a long time to sink in. It was hard to let go of the hard knot of fear in the pit of my stomach that had rested there like a constant companion, giving hourly meaning to my life. The sounds of celebration around our camping area sounded half-hearted and unconvincing. The victory felt empty, It didn't feel 'right' to have survived so many battles. I also felt resentful that many Germans around us had been rescued from the death they deserved.

There were sad handshakes and hugs around camp, as we packed up the next day and moved into Gilgenberg, Austria, about forty miles north of Salzberg, where we were greeted by a unit of Russian infantry. The Russians were cheering as they ran toward us with huge grins and with bottles of vodka extended to us. We spoke our respective languages at each other without a concern for translation. Stringed instruments appeared along with harmonicas, as everyone began dancing in the street. A giant Russian soldier grabbed me and began to dance. This hulking form wrapped in padded winter clothing proved to be a woman soldier, who roared with laughter at my awkward attempts to follow her lead.

Townspeople joined in the celebration. Young girls of the town, in bright dresses showered hugs and kisses on us but stayed clear of the Russians. A few shots of vodka helped me to get into the spirit of the celebration. We exchanged gifts of food and souvenirs. I had my first taste of caviar and loved it. Non-fraternization rules were now null and void. One pretty girl invited Jerry into her home. As he walked off with her, grinning from ear to ear he shouted, "Hey Andy, see you later. Looks like I had to go half way 'round the world to get laid." We moved into the buildings of the town for a night and welcomed the arrival of mail from home. The Russians and friendly Austrians had shaken us out of our depressions for the moment.

For the next couple of days we were all in a kind of daze. German soldiers were everywhere, trying to surrender. Some units just marched up the middle of the road between our truck and tank columns heading to our rear. Our instinctual alertness resulted in some German soldiers being shot, as they would step out of buildings unexpectedly. A whistle of any kind would find us dropping to the ground or diving for a low spot. We became the police of whatever town we were in and spent most our time on guard duty. Hot meals became the order of the day and our mess sergeant, Steele, was grinning his evil grin but without the usual hostile barbs. He seemed intimidated by our dirty, blood soaked appearance, even acknowledging that we must have had a bad time of it.

I was concerned that my family didn't know I had survived the final days of the war. I knew that a letter I had just written would take forever to reach them. I also wrote another letter to Danielle, in care of the military hospital in Le Havre, to let her know that the Germans had not destroyed her good work in saving my life. I thanked her again for helping get me back to the 86th. I told her of my hope to see her again. I was shocked to realize that it had been only two months since I was in the hospital. It seemed like years. Chester said he would make sure the letter got to her. I also gave him the latest letters from Mom whom he also called Mom now. She had also sent him a picture of herself with Dad, and one of our home.

That same day several of us contacted our friend, Chaplain Sanders, about a way to get word to our families. He spoke of official chaplain channels which would speed things up. With a wry smile, he said if we were to be baptized by him he could send a baptismal notice, including the post cease-fire date through government routes to our homes, so our families would know we made it. Jerry bargained with the Chaplain. He agreed to be baptized if the Chaplain would just notify his parents that he was alive and not mention the ceremony. We went with Sanders to a stream on the edge of the town of Mattsee. Needing a bath anyway, we all dived into the icy water. One by one he immersed us, except Jerry, with a brief statement of baptism and then headed back to the radio tent to send word back to the States. We heard that today was the official VE day, May 8th. We also heard for the first time that Hitler and his girlfriend had killed themselves in Berlin.

Without the ever-present enemy and attack orders, we were lost. The beauty and peacefulness of Austria was annoying. I felt angry as I watched the people of the town return to business as usual. In fact, everyone except Chester were 'down' and short-tempered. Chester's home would be the regular army. That's where he was happy. He would go anywhere. He was oblivious to the absence of artillery, mud, icy rain, and death. Peace was intolerable and the warm air and bright sunlight was unbearable. Fights kept breaking out over stupid little things, like snoring. The end had come too quickly. I found myself looking around for friends who were dead. I kept an eye out for Brewster, even though he was dead. Hitler and Mussolini were dead. Roosevelt was dead. Some guy named Harry Truman was now my president and I didn't even know who he was. We had won the war in

Europe, but victory was disturbing. I was living in another world, angry and depressed.

One evening, Jerry and I were quietly cleaning our weapons when a knife fight broke out between Sergeant Steele and Kraus. They called it off when they realized that none of us was trying to stop them. I told Jerry I was disappointed that they didn't keep at it. Jerry observed wisely, "Looks like we get along better when somebody's shooting at us."

"Jerry, it's worse than that with me. I want to kill some more. Like it's not finished for me. Before Dachau I killed to stay alive. Since then, I looked forward to the killing. Something's wrong with me."

"Naw, it's the same with me Andy. I think you were more shocked by what you saw than I was. You didn't grow up in a New York ghetto. You didn't experience being hated just because you were Swedish. I like your outrage, Andy. Because of it you probably took more chances than I did, and killed more of them."

"Jerry, I grew up hating killing. For forty two days I killed someone almost everyday. I've crossed over into some other kind of dimension. I have feelings I don't know what to do with. I'm a killer. I didn't want to be but I am. I enjoy it. That's unforgivable."

"Calm down Andy. I'm with you. I feel the same. I just keep telling myself that somebody had to stop the fucking Germans and we were drafted to do it. Just remember how many millions of people they tortured and killed."

"That helps Jerry. Thanks. Are you going to talk about how it was and what we did when you get home?"

"Probably not, Andy. You know me. I'll tell my cynical, sarcastic stories and make everybody laugh."

"You do know Jerry, that we're not normal anymore don't you? I'll just go home and pretend to be normal. I will never tell the truth about this to anyone at home. They would be grateful that I helped win the war but would see me as a kind of monster. Nope! I will put it all away, forever. Just the funny parts, that's what I'll talk about."

After about two days of this, Colonel King came to our rescue. Standing in his jeep equipped with a field PA system, he told us that we were leaving the Third Army and were now attached to the 15th Corps of the 7th Army. Then he said he had some good news and some bad news. The good news was a letter he had received from the commander of the Third Corps, which listed all of our accomplishments in forty-two days of combat. He was recommending that all of us with Combat Infantry Badges be awarded a Bronze Star.

Jerry got a roar of approval as he shouted, "Sir, does that mean we get a raise?"

King decided to ignore the comment and proceeded with more good news. "We will leave immediately for Camp Old Gold and then to Le Havre to board a troop ship for home. We will be the first combat division to return to the States and a thirty day furlough." Our Colonel waited for the cheering to stop.

Then he proceeded, "Now the bad news. After our furlough we will be re-equipped and given brush-up training at Camp Gruber, Oklahoma, for action in the South Pacific. Probably the invasion of Japan." I joined in the moans and groans after a brief, shocked silence. After being dismissed we grouped together with our remaining buddies to chew over this latest twist of fate. Most of us as A.S.T.P.ers immediately recalled the formation in Fort Benning when we were delivered into the infantry instead of into a college.

Colonel King hung around a bit chatting with our officers and then came over to me. "Sorry, Corporal. I wish to hell I was sending you guys home."

"Thanks, Colonel." Then changing the subject, I asked about his scalp.

He took off his helmet and said, "It doesn't really hurt anymore." He lifted the bandage still wrapped around his head and said, "Want to see your handiwork?" I took a look and found that healing was nearly complete with no infections. He said that Marty had removed his stitches and put them in a little pouch for him as a souvenir. "Oh," he said, pausing, as he was walking off, "Read the casualty list and saw that our friend Brewster finally got it. Guess we can both breath easier now." That was the first time I realized that Colonel King had also been worried about getting shot in the back by Brewster. The parting words of the man who had led us for forty-two days of combat was, "I'm sorry I won't be with you in the South Pacific. I'm being promoted and reassigned stateside. Good luck soldier."

The next day, as our convoy of trucks moved out of our little town heading north and west, most of the population was already on the road, and moving out with us to avoid the vengeful Russian occupation. Jerry was wearing a happy face for a change and from his 'thumbs up,' I knew he had obviously had a good time with his Austrian girlfriend. I re-read the letter I had received from Danielle and tried to think of ways to see her before we left. Everyone on my truck wanted to help, but all hope faded with the realization that there would be not be any opportunities to slip away. We were on a bee-line course for our ship in Le Havre. Jerry also reminded me that I didn't need another Court Martial.

On the very day that we boarded the troop ship, USAT General Parker, in the Port of Le Havre, a telegram arrived in the mailbox at our ranch outside of Kingsburg, thousands of miles away. Mom and Dad had walked together to get the mail and found an ominous looking envelope from The War Department, Office Of The Chaplain. Neither dared open it immediately as they walked slowly to sit under a tree in the orange grove. Fearing the worst, they began to open the envelope as they agreed it must be about me as my brother was still safe on Guam. With an arm around each other and expecting to read, "By now you have received the sad news that your son was killed in action…", they were stunned and dissolved in tears as they read instead, my baptismal notice, dated the day after V-E Day.

Home again

BRINGING HOME AN OLD FRIEND

The concrete gun store with security bars on its painted windows and the forbidding, black iron door had lost none of its bleakness in the two years since my previous visit. However, as I parked my car and approached the entrance, it was without the dread I felt last time. This time there was just excitement. I opened the iron door and stepped into the gun-filled room that still reeked of cordite, cosmolene and after-shave lotion. All of the salesmen except Vince were leaning over pistol cases, deep in quiet conversations. A warm, playful smile spread over his face when he saw me come in.

"Andy! I'll be damned!" he shouted. "You came back! We got your check a long time ago so I just put your M-1 away for you. You here to pick it up?"

"Yeah, finally." I replied as we shook hands. "I guess I'm ready for it now. You really pulled the plug on my memories when I was here last time, Vince. Thanks to you and your questions it all started coming back —including the nightmares. I took your advice and started telling my wife and kids. I also started writing down everything I could remember. My writing teacher and class think it should be a book."

"Just wish my Dad had told me more," Vince replied as he stepped into a back room to bring out my rifle. When he handed it to me I could see it was cleaned for firing. All metal parts were gleaming with a thin coat of oil. No chunks of cosmolene were left. The coloration of the wooden stock and the two handguards were slightly mismatched, just like the rifle I had carried in the war. I opened the bolt and carefully depressed the clip follower with my thumb to allow the bolt to snap closed. Vince watched closely and with relief said, "I see you haven't forgotten how to get your thumb out of the way when you close the bolt."

"One smashed thumb in basic training was all I needed," I replied. Vince prowled through a nearby display case and came back with an M-1 bayonet and scabbard and a leather sling.

"You'll probably want these if you're gonna have a real keepsake," he declared as he expertly installed the sling and snapped the bayonet onto the rifle barrel, removing the scabbard as he did so. He presented me with the fully-equipped rifle and said, "Andy, here's the best friend you ever had." He obviously knew that the concept of our rifle as our best friend was drummed into the brain of combat infantryman over and over again, and that the truth of that statement was proven in battle.

As I held the rifle, now sporting a bayonet, Vince asked, "Remember bayonet drill?

"I think so," I answered, as my body dropped into a crouch with my right hand on the forward barrel guard and my left hand gripping the stock. I lunged forward with my right leg ahead and extended both arms into a 'long thrust.' Then, as if I had hit my target with the bayonet, I now moved my left hand up behind my right hand and withdrew the blade. Then, re-gripping the stock as before, I pushed the butt of the rifle into an upward arc called a 'butt-stroke,' aimed at an imaginary chin. I followed that with a reverse of the arc into a downward 'slash' at an invisible neck.

"That's damned good. Ever kill anybody that way?"

"No, I was lucky. My big fear in combat was running out of ammo and having to use that damn thing. God, it's been a long time."

I decided to buy the bayonet and sling and also some thirty caliber ammunition. Vince threw in a cleaning kit and patches that fit into a couple of holes behind a metal flap door on the butt of the rifle.

"What are you going to do with this thing," Vince asked. I told him how I planned to make a display case in my den and hang it up as a souvenier.

"But before that there's one final thing I have to do. I have to see what happens when I actually shoot it again. My son, Mark, is taking me to a rifle range in the hills of San Luis Obispo."

"Good idea," Vince said as slipped the rifle into a plastic bag. "Remember how an M1 has a kind of soft popping sound compared to the "bang" of most rifles? Oh, and don't forget to keep the butt tight to your shoulder. It has a pretty good kick."

I picked up the rifle and the bag of equipment, shook hands and said, "Thanks for everything. Guess it's time to take my old friend home."On the way home, the presence of the M-1 in the trunk of my car overshadowed everything else. My mind, usually scattered over a vast number of issues, was locked on one incredible thought. *I own an M-1 rifle like the one I carried in the war.*

With great ceremony I unveiled the rifle, bayonet and ammunition for my wife, Celia. Dinner was delayed while I introduced her to my prize by demonstrating the manual of arms, bayonet drill and field-stripping. With the bayonet attached, I leaned it against a wall while we had dinner and marveled at how much larger and heavier it was than I remembered. We couldn't keep our eyes off of it. It looked deadly and intimidating. When I moved it to another room, it continued to enforce its ominous presence. I took pictures of it. We showed it to neighbors and friends who came by. I took it through the West Point Academy Dress Manual of Arms. I handled it almost every time I went by it and found myself talking to it as if we were old buddies who had let a close friendship lapse.

Comfort finally settled in. I bought a book on the history of the M-1 and all of its descendants. Our reunion was going well. It did its part too. It quietly evoked more memories of training and combat experiences for my writing. My old friend and I were about ready for the grand finale...a day on the rifle range.

On the way to San Luis Obispo, my enthusiasm began to fade. My son, Mark, was ready with some antique rifles and pistols he wanted to check out. He had made arrangements for the use of a rifle range north of town, just across from Camp San Luis Obispo, where I was stationed before leaving for Europe in 1944. As we got under way, Mark's eagerness to shoot an M-1 for the first time only increased the tightness in my stomach.

At Camp San Luis Obispo we stopped briefly to look at the layout of the Army camp. It was still occupied by a military unit. The rows and rows of white painted tar-paper huts, paved streets, parade grounds and bustling army trucks, sprawled in front of the Seven Sisters mountain range. The brilliant green grass that I remembered from the winter of '44 was now dry and brown. We enjoyed the coincidence that his school, Cuesta College, was built on a portion of the Camp property. The former location of my tar-paper hut was in the middle of Mark's college campus. I told him that I liked the idea of a college growing out of the ruins of my old army camp and that my son was a student there.

We turned north and east off of the highway we were on a twisting, hilly road into more mountains, where my 86th Division Blackhawks had practiced combat assaults. Just when we ran out of paved road we began to hear the crackling sounds of rifle fire. "Deja Vu, eh Dad? We even have the rifle fire for you." The 'cracking' gunfire loosened the tightness in my stomach. The familiarity of that sound along with seeing the row of shooters, and metal targets instead of enemy soldiers brought relief. After parking and being greeted by the range manager, a friend of my son's, we took our place in a row of weather-beaten redwood shooting tables. Mark readied a 45-70 caliber, 1885 Browning rifle and I took my M-1 out of the blanket it was wrapped in.

Having nodded a greeting, the men at the other tables paused to watch as I loaded some M-1 clips with eight rounds each and shoved one into the rifle. As the bolt closed, carrying the first shell into the chamber, I settled into a basic firing position. The other shooters, who had paused to watch as I readied my rifle, returned to their own, reassured that I knew what I was doing.

Mark insisted that I take the shooting stool first. The field in front of our firing line was grassy with a high ridge at the far end to absorb the bullets that missed targets. Scattered throughout the field were various shaped rusty iron figures of animals, each one swinging on chains.

"Dad, how long since you shot an M-1?" Mark asked.

"About fifty-seven years. Guess that's why I feel a little nervous." With both elbows on the table and the rifle stock pulled snugly against my left shoulder to avoid bruises, those years evaporated. I was suddenly on the rifle range at Fort Benning.

The Rangemaster's voice barked over the loudspeaker, "Ready on the left,—Ready on the right,—Ready on the firing line. Comeeeeeence—firing!"

As I began to squeeze the trigger, I realized that the metal gorilla I was aiming at was two hundred yards away. I hadn't adjusted the sight. From some distant memory I knew to turn the elevation knob three clicks up and made no adjustment sideways for windage since no wind was blowing.

I settled into aiming stance again, took several deep breaths, let out half of the last one and slowly squeezed the trigger. A shadowy sniper appeared in the center of my sight, hiding in a balcony in the middle of a fire-fight. Rifle and machine gun fire was all around me. My rifle spurted fire with the familiar muffled "pop," and slammed into my shoulder. Instead of seeing the sniper pitch forward onto the bloody cobbled street, I heard a metallic clink as the gorilla squeaked back and forth on its chains. My second shot also hit the target. Mark retrieved the two shell casings and put them in his pocket.

"When was the last time you fired an M-1?" he asked.

I thought for a minute, hesitant to answer. Then I asked, "The truth?" When he nodded, I said, "On my final patrol in the Philippines, where we went after Europe. I shot a Japanese soldier charging out of his cave right at us—his rifle had jammed." We were both silent. I dropped the rifle on the table. Then I picked it up, only to drop it again. As I moved to pick it up once more, I thought, *so here it is. My grand finale. What do I do with this damn thing that I just had to have*. I wanted to avoid it, like an old friend who knows too much about you.

Mark said, "Dad, if you want to stop and go home that's really O.K. with me."

Calmed by my son's compassion I said, "No, I think it would be best if we shot up all the ammo we have and then we'll go."

Mark grinned. "All right!" He began firing his antique and I went through several more clips of shells. I could hear a voice in my head, probably speaking for all of my traumatized therapy clients saying, "Just face your demons from the past and they will go away." More combat images came and went, stimulated by the hot rifle in my hands, by the gunfire all around, by the rolling clouds of gunsmoke and by an increasingly sore shoulder. During the last two clips no more images appeared..

While cleaning our rifles, Mark drew an oily patch through his and said soberly, "I've got another question."

"What is it?"

"Well, you know I've read everything you've written, several times, and I was wondering…" He paused, then continued. "Well, with all the killing, the close calls and being shot at and all, —is it with you all the time, now that you've brought it all back?"

"Well, it is, but the writing, and reading it to Celia and my writing class, and just talking about it like we are now has made it easier to live with. Like nightmares when we share them. I guess I have a new kind of respect for what I went through." He was clearly glad to hear this.

Then he asked, "Is there something that especially haunts you and won't go away?"

"Yeah, there is," I answered slowly. "The look on the face of the first man I killed."

Mark just nodded sadly as I picked up the rifle, which now seemed lighter. As we climbed into his pick-up, Mark broke the silence, "So, what are you going to do with it? Put it away or hang it on the wall with the Civil War rifle I gave you?"

"I don't know yet. It may have served its purpose. I don't want to be ashamed of it, or of myself for what we had to do, but I don't think I want to see it on my wall everyday. Guess we'll have to wait and see." While saying goodby, I said, "I'm glad I could share this with you today Son, You helped me get rid of some more demons."

He smiled and said, "Just promise me something Dad,—that you'll keep on writing."

Two week later I opened a small package from Mark. In it was a shiny brass, ball-point pen that had been hand-crafted out of the first two shells I had fired in my M-1.

**ROUTE OF THE 86th
BLACKHAWK DIVISION**
MARCH 4, TO JUNE 7, 1945

GERMANY

Hagen

RUHR VALLEY

Cologne

Aachen / Bonn

Rhine

Frankfurt

Wurzburg

Nuremberg

FRANCE

Danube

Ingolstadt

Dachau

Munich

Salzburg

SWITZERLAND

AUSTRIA

Printed in the United States
90500LV00007B/41/A